Core Competencies in the Solution-Focused and Strategic Therapies

Core Competencies in Psychotherapy Series

SERIES EDITOR
Len Sperry
Florida Atlantic University, Medical College of Wisconsin

Competency represents a paradigm shift in the training and practice of psychotherapy that is already challenging much of what is familiar and comfortable. This series addresses the core competencies common to highly effective psychotherapeutic practice and includes individual volumes for the most commonly practiced approaches today: cognitive behavior, brief dynamic and solution focused therapies, and others.

VOLUMES IN THIS SERIES

Core Competencies in the Solution-Focused and Strategic Therapies

Becoming a Highly Competent Solution-Focused and Strategic Therapist

ELLEN K. QUICK

Routledge
Taylor & Francis Group
New York   London

Routledge
Taylor & Francis Group
711 Third Avenue
New York, NY 10017

Routledge
Taylor & Francis Group
27 Church Road
Hove, East Sussex BN3 2FA

© 2012 by Taylor & Francis Group, LLC
Routledge is an imprint of Taylor & Francis Group, an Informa business

Printed in the United States of America on acid-free paper
Version Date: 20110705

International Standard Book Number: 978-0-415-88530-0 (Paperback)

Library of Congress Cataloging-in-Publication Data

Quick, Ellen Kaufman.
  Core competencies in the solution-focused and strategic therapies : becoming a highly competent solution-focused and strategic therapist / by Ellen K. Quick.
      p. ; cm. -- (Core competencies in psychotherapy series)
  Includes bibliographical references and index.
  ISBN 978-0-415-88530-0 (pbk. : alk. paper)
    1. Solution-focused therapy. 2. Strategic therapy. 3. Core competencies. I. Title. II. Series: Core competencies in psychotherapy series (New York, N.Y.)
    [DNLM: 1. Clinical Competence. 2. Psychotherapy, Brief--methods. 3.Outcome and Process Assessment (Health Care) WM 21]

  RC489.S65Q53 2011
  616.89'147--dc23   2011019125

Visit the Taylor & Francis Web site at
http://www.taylorandfrancis.com

and the Routledge Web site at
http://www.routledgementalhealth.com

CONTENTS

CONTENTS

FOREWORD

When Ellen Quick approached me during the 2010 European Brief Therapy Association (EBTA) Conference in Malmo, Sweden, asking me to write a foreword to her forthcoming book on competencies in the solution-focused and strategic therapies, I gave an enthusiastic "yes." Having met Ellen at various EBTA conferences and having read her book on strategic solution focused therapy, I knew what a sharp thinker she is. Also, I knew that we work along similar lines, trying to promote a flexible and integrative "hybrid"—as she calls it—way to understand solution-focused work. But then, on second thought, I found that I had some reservations. As a university person, I know how boring the literature on competencies can be and how easily it can slip into bureaucratic, confusing jargon.

Some months later, when I read the manuscript, I realized how unwarranted my worries had been. Ellen had produced—again—a very interesting text, brilliantly written, easy to read, and full of relevant clinical examples that illustrate "real therapy" and give a vivid account of clinical practice. In fact, the book sparked so many ideas and reflections that I find it difficult to condense them in a brief foreword. I would like to start by stating that Ellen Quick's combination of the strategic and solution-focused perspectives is an excellent way to do justice to the historical and conceptual continuity that exists between the two approaches. Although the solution-focused model evolved from Mental Research Institute (MRI) strategic therapy (I do remember Steve de Shazer wondering, during session breaks, what homework task John Weakland would suggest), the two approaches are sometimes perceived to be at odds: "Problem talk" sometimes appears to be "forbidden" in solution-focused practice, and some strategic therapists seem to ignore solution-focused ideas. The strategic solution focused model that Ellen proposes is an outstanding example of how to think in "both–and" instead of in "either–or" terms and of how to do so without getting too complex or losing therapeutic creativity.

In addition, accepting that "one size will not fit all," Ellen Quick adds very interesting elements to standard strategic and solution-focused practice. And she does it without leaving the conceptual playground of solution-focused and strategic theoretical premises. As a researcher on therapeutic processes, I appreciate Ellen's explicit acknowledgement of the value of the therapeutic alliance in brief therapy. She not only recognizes the important role of the alliance as an outcome predictor but also shows how solution-focused and strategic techniques and attitudes actively contribute to a strong alliance. Her discussion of the stages of change model opens the option of acknowledging and using clients' ambivalence toward change, a topic that is usually neglected in straightforward solution-focused literature. And Ellen's advocacy of therapeutic transparency is a welcome antidote to the more manipulative flavor that strategic therapy can have when performed in an unskilled manner. Another important asset of the strategic solution focused model is that the "do more of what works; change what does not" philosophy is transformed into advice that can be offered to clients. This psychoeducational element of Ellen's work might seem at odds with the cherished "not-knowing" position of solution-focused therapists, but it makes a lot of sense in the real world of therapy, where therapists are often expected to bring in not only their procedural knowledge on therapeutic conversations but also some direct advice for their clients.

The analysis of solution-focused and strategic therapy in terms of therapeutic competencies yields a number of interesting outcomes. It provides a more nuanced view of solution-focused and strategic practice, as it distinguishes the performance of novice, advanced beginner, competent, proficient, and expert practitioners. Conceptually, this is more constructive than the simple dichotomy between good and bad or between "solution-focused" and "solution-forced" therapy. The discussion of various degrees of competence will allow solution-focused and strategic trainers to anticipate possible difficulties in the learning process of their trainees. It will also help researchers to spell out criteria for competence and proficiency, an issue that is certainly relevant in the evaluation of treatment integrity and adherence. In this way, the dissemination of strategic and solution-focused practices in academic settings is also made easier.

This book also builds bridges between the solution-focused and strategic therapies and the more problem- and diagnosis-oriented world of clinical psychology and behavioral healthcare agencies. Solution-focused therapists do not usually talk about their "case conceptualizations" or their "integrative diagnostic assessments," but Ellen shows how this language can be used without putting solution-focused theories at risk. In addition, dialogue with other approaches is promoted. Concepts like "resolving transference and countertransference" and "repairing therapeutic alliances," foreign to many brief therapists, are discussed in a solution-focused and strategic way. This promotes collaboration with the broader community of psychotherapists, as does Ellen's willingness to integrate procedures like mindfulness, dialectical behavior therapy, and acceptance and commitment therapy.

A number of challenges remain. Some differences between strategic and solution-focused therapy may seem more "irreconcilable" (to quote one of Insoo Kim Berg's published cases [Berg, 2008]) than others. For instance, the MRI concept of "second-order change" may appear to be inconsistent with the solution-focused emphasis on progressive, cumulative change, and the "strategizing" and "leading from behind" positions may seem irreconcilable. Another challenge is how far one wants to go in the direction of using specific therapeutic procedures for specific populations or problem types, as strategic authors such as Nardone and his colleagues (Nardone & Watzlawick, 1993; Nardone & Portelli, 2005) have done. Ellen Quick proposes an elegant way to integrate different procedures, inviting therapists to use empirically supported treatments in a strategic way (Would this be a 180-degree change in regard to this client's attempted solutions?) and/or in a solution-focused manner (Is this client already doing some of it?), always staying attuned to clients' feedback and unique needs. Perhaps, as in Berg's session, differences that initially appear to be irreconcilable can be approached in a way that invites collaboration.

I am confident that this book will be a valuable resource for many different readers. For the newcomer to strategic or solution-focused therapy, it provides an excellent way to get started, without losing sight of the broader context of general psychotherapeutic principles and practices. A seasoned solution-focused or strategic practitioner will find a stimulating and fresh view of his or her preferred practices, as well as new ideas and invitations to expand one's therapeutic resources. For trainers in solution-focused and strategic therapy, *Core Competencies in the Solution-Focused and Strategic Therapies* offers an expanded map of the training process in these approaches, with precise language to describe the competencies involved. And for psychotherapy researchers, it offers a wide array of hypotheses to be tested. One could hardly ask for more!

Mark Beyebach, PhD
Director, Master's Programme in Family Therapy and Systemic Intervention
Universidad Pontificia de Salamanca, Spain

PREFACE

When I am not conducting psychotherapy, I can often be found making music. I play the Celtic harp, mostly solo, and soprano, alto, tenor, and bass recorders, mostly with my recorder ensemble. As a serious amateur, I sometimes perform but primarily play for pleasure; I also strive to improve my playing. During the process of thinking and writing about competency in the domain of psychotherapy, I have also reflected about the different competencies involved in playing instrumental music. In doing so, I have realized more clearly something that, on some level, I already knew: For any individual musician, as for any individual therapist, some competencies grow more quickly and easily, and others take more effort and practice. For example, I sight-read recorder sheet music comfortably—in the language of this book, at the level of adequate competency—but I remain at the lower levels of competency when sight-reading on the harp. I memorize new pieces quickly and easily on the harp but not on the recorder. And without deliberate effort, I will tend to do more of what comes easily and avoid what is more difficult.

The same phenomenon emerges for us as psychotherapists. As a supervisor of predoctoral clinical psychology interns, I regularly see developing psychologists who begin the internship year with variable skills in different domains. One intern may already be competent at forming relationships, but she may be an advanced beginner in terms of familiarity with solution-focused and strategic methods. Another may have learned and practiced many techniques while still being a beginner in "stretching his flexibility muscles" when something is not working well enough. By the end of the internship year, the goal is for all interns to display competency for basic practice in multiple domains, with increased awareness of areas where they will want to create opportunities for more deliberate practice—and excitement about building advancing proficiency in areas of special interest and expertise.

When Len Sperry approached me about writing this book, my initial reaction was that the recent second edition of *Doing What Works in Brief Therapy: A Strategic Solution Focused Approach* (Quick, 2008) had already addressed the topic. I quickly realized, however, that that this was not the case. Like most books about psychotherapy models, *Doing What Works in*

Brief Therapy describes a set of *methods*. In contrast, this book addresses the *competencies* needed to use a method and how to enhance them.

Competency means being capable of something, and it is comprised of *knowledge*, *skills*, and *attitudes*. As described in more detail in Chapter 1, competency in specific domains is increasingly being demanded by multiple behavioral healthcare disciplines, by employers, and by consumers of psychotherapy. In a world where there is increasing insistence on "evidence-based practice," demonstrating competence is a critical component. A "culture of competence" is emerging in both training and clinical practice.

This book is part of Routledge's *Core Competencies in Psychotherapy* series. The two introductory books in this series introduce the competency perspective and discuss twenty clinical competencies. One of these, *Core Competencies in Counseling and Psychotherapy: Becoming a Highly Competent and Effective Therapist* (Sperry, 2010a), emphasizes the knowledge and attitudinal components. The other, *Highly Effective Therapy: Developing Essential Clinical Competencies in Counseling and Psychotherapy* (Sperry, 2010b), focuses on the skills component.

This book is one of three at the next "tier," which includes a separate volume on each of the three primary methods of psychotherapy being practiced today. According to Sperry, these methods are (a) cognitive behavioral, (b) psychodynamic, and (c) solution-focused and strategic psychotherapy. This book covers the core competencies in the solution-focused and strategic therapies and discusses how to become a more proficient solution-focused and strategic therapist.

Chapter 1 of this volume introduces the competency perspective and presents the core competencies. Chapters 2 through 10 describe how the solution-focused and strategic therapies approach each of the 20 clinical competencies introduced in Chapter 1. One of these competencies involves learning and applying a conceptual map. Discussion of the conceptual framework summarizes the seminal work done at the Mental Research Institute (MRI) and later at the Brief Family Therapy Center (BFTC), and it describes an integrated strategic solution focused approach.

Five competencies address the therapeutic relationship, with emphasis on both relationship development and relationship maintenance. Five additional competencies focus on intervention planning, with four others emphasizing implementation of interventions. Two competencies cover evaluation of interventions and termination, and three address culturally and ethically sensitive practice. Chapter 11 discusses ways of enhancing competency in solution-focused and strategic therapy, with discussion of how the therapist can move from "minimal competency" to higher levels of proficiency.

Throughout the book, each competency is viewed through the "lens" of solution-focused and strategic observation and thinking. There is an emphasis on tailoring treatment to clients' unique strengths and preferences, with the client determining the area for change and the goal. An important cluster of skills and attitudes focuses on respectful, careful, accurate listening, sometimes called *leading from behind*. There is an emphasis on discovering and amplifying what works and changing what does not work—both in the client's life and in the therapist's process.

Solution-focused and strategic therapists are a diverse group. I use a model that deliberately integrates solution-focused and strategic theory and methods. Many other systemic therapists, both those who are primarily solution-focused and those who are primarily strategic, also blend approaches and use components of the models together. Others may bristle at the implication that the same book that describes "their" approach is also describing the "other one." I have attempted to convey an attitude of respect for the diversity within the international community of solution-focused and strategic therapists. Just as one size does not fit all for clients, there are both commonalities and differences in the knowledge, skills, and attitudes emphasized by different members of the systemic therapy "family."

The primary audience for this book is the psychotherapist. It is written for practitioners from all of the behavioral healthcare disciplines and at all levels of training. For readers who are experienced practitioners of the solution-focused and strategic therapies, this book will help them to "translate" what they are already doing into the competency-based "language spoken" in an increasing number of training and practice settings. The book will be useful for beginning therapists and the faculty and supervisors who guide them; it also will assist seasoned practitioners in recognizing and amplifying ways of moving to higher levels of competency in their solution-focused and strategic practice.

Some readers of this book may be more familiar with cognitive behavioral and psychodynamic models than with the solution-focused and strategic perspective described in this book. As these readers learn about an approach that is new to them, they will discover the power of "extreme listening and observing," building on strengths, amplifying what works, and doing something different. And they will learn that the solution-focused and strategic therapies are not just a set of methods but a matrix of knowledge, skills, and attitudes.

This book will also be of interest to faculty in the behavioral health-care disciplines, particularly those who would like to introduce psychotherapy models in a way that resonates with the competency-based criteria in their own programs and in their disciplines. The book will be used primarily at the graduate level, but it will be useful in advanced undergraduate coursework as well. Training directors of internships, practica, and residencies; behavioral healthcare administrators and managers; and policy makers will also find the book of interest. Psychotherapy researchers will find this book useful for planning quantitative and qualitative research to add to the growing evidence base on process and outcome in the solution-focused and strategic therapies.

The knowledge, guidance, and support of many people have made this book possible. My work with Milton Erickson, with the MRI faculty (Richard Fisch in particular), and with the BFTC (Steve de Shazer, Insoo Kim Berg) profoundly influenced my thinking. On several occasions Scott Miller brought solution-focused training to my colleagues in San Diego, and that led to the growth of a supportive community of solution-focused and strategic practice here, particularly the San Diego Strategic Solution Focused Professional Interest group of the 1990s. My friends and colleagues at the Kaiser Permanente Department of Psychiatry and Addiction Medicine, the Solution-Focused Brief Therapy Association (SFBTA), and the European Brief Therapy Association (EBTA) continue to provide me with stimulation, support, and community.

I would like to thank Mark Beyebach for writing the Foreword. His thoughtful comments add a valuable perspective from an academic center of systemic research and training on the other side of the globe.

I want to express my appreciation to Len Sperry for his vision in creating the *Core Competencies in Psychotherapy* series and for inviting my participation. George Zimmar, Marta Moldvai, and David Tumarkin at Routledge have provided valuable support.

I also would like to acknowledge the publishers who have kindly provided permission to reprint and/or adapt previously published material in this book: Taylor & Francis Books for *More Than Miracles: The State of the Art of Solution-Focused Brief Therapy* (de Shazer & Dolan, 2007) and *Highly Effective Therapy: Developing Essential Clinical Competencies in Counseling and Psychotherapy* (Sperry, 2010b); Elsevier for *Doing What Works in Brief Therapy: A Strategic Solution Focused Approach* (2nd ed.; Quick, 2008); and

John Wiley & Sons, Inc., for *Brief Therapy With Intimidating Cases* (Fisch & Schlanger, 1999).

I want to thank my clients. You have an amazing capacity to discover the strengths within you and to build on them in creative ways that I could not have imagined, and you do it even in the most difficult of circumstances. You remind me both to return to the basics and to do something different. You are teaching me all the time.

Finally, I want to thank my daughter, Melissa, and my husband, Frank, for your humor, support, and love. Your presence is invaluable.

My thanks to all of you.

Ellen K. Quick, PhD

ABOUT THE AUTHOR

Ellen K. Quick, PhD, is a clinical psychologist who specializes in brief psychotherapy. She earned a bachelor's degree from Wellesley College (1970)
and a doctorate in clinical psychology from the University of Pittsburgh
(1974). Since 1981, she has practiced at Kaiser Permanente in San Diego.
Dr. Quick trained at the Mental Research Institute, at the Brief Family
Therapy Center, and with Milton Erickson. She has written and taught
about the integration of solution-focused and strategic therapy, with an
emphasis on "doing what works" on multiple levels: in the client's life, in
the therapist's work, and as a philosophy shared with the client.

1

Introducing the Clinical Competencies of the Solution-Focused and Strategic Therapies

Competency is an exciting focus in psychotherapy training and practice today. It is not simply a set of standards or an educational method; rather, it is a different way of approaching teaching, learning, supervision, and continuing professional development. Multiple behavioral healthcare disciplines increasingly emphasize competency-based training. In clinical psychology and marriage and family therapy, both graduate programs and internships now routinely define and assess competency in multiple domains. As Sperry (2010a) pointed out, psychiatry training programs require residents to demonstrate competency in at least three approaches to psychotherapy.

This chapter begins with key definitions of competency-related terms and describes the three components of a competency: knowledge, skill, and attitude. It introduces the six core competencies and the related 20 essential clinical competencies, and it describes the five developmental stages of expertise/competency in psychotherapy training and practice. The chapter also provides an overview of the remaining chapters, which discuss and illustrate these competencies in the solution-focused and strategic therapies.

What are core competencies in psychotherapy in general, and in solution-focused and strategic therapy in particular? And why does this matter to solution-focused and strategic therapists? This chapter addresses those questions. Solution-focused and strategic therapies emphasize "doing what works and changing what does not" at multiple levels: in the client's life, in the therapist's process, and as a philosophy that is collaboratively shared with the client. Highly competent solution-focused and strategic therapists "lead from behind," amplify client strengths, and shift gears when something is not working well enough. They may not, however, think of these skills as "competencies."

Until now, the "language of competencies" has not regularly been "spoken" in training and practice in the solution-focused and strategic therapies. This book changes that. Solution-focused and strategic therapists know how important it is to identify the "customer," to join with the client, and to speak the client's language (both figuratively and literally). Today, in the psychotherapy and behavioral healthcare world of the early 21st century, the customer increasingly wants, even demands, "evidence-based practice," which includes "practice-based evidence" (a concept discussed in more detail later in this book). Just as computer literacy and knowledge of managed care are increasingly in the therapist's toolbox, the language of core competencies is a language that solution-focused and strategic therapists need to speak.

DEFINITION OF COMPETENCIES
AND THEIR COMPONENTS

The dictionary definition of *competence* refers to being capable of something or qualified for some role by education or training (Funk & Wagnells, 1966, p. 276). Referring to competence in the behavioral healthcare domains, Sperry (2010b) offered the following definition:

> Competence has been defined as the consistent and judicious use of knowledge, technical skills, clinical reasoning, emotions, values, and reflection in clinical practice. Competence involves the capacity for critical thinking, analysis, and professional judgment in assessing a situation and making clinical decisions based on that assessment. Furthermore, it is the ability to evaluate and modify one's decisions, as appropriate,

through reflective practice (Kaslow, 2004). Clinical competencies are composed of three interrelated components, knowledge, skills, and attitudes, which are essential for effective professional practice. Such competencies are reflected in the quality of clinical performance, can be evaluated against professional standards, and can be developed or enhanced through professional training and personal growth (Kaslow, 2004). (Sperry, 2010b, p. 2)

Kaslow (2004) pointed out that the term competence is sometimes used to imply a minimum threshold. This is the case when credentialing bodies require minimal competencies for one to be considered a professional. However, she added that a competency-based approach also refers to a more aspirational striving toward excellence. Those who achieve the higher levels of competence in a field are often considered to be the "experts."

As noted above, competencies include three components: (a) knowledge, (b) skills, and (c) attitudes. *Knowledge* refers to the conceptual foundation for one's practice. It grows from formal training and study, in graduate school and beyond. One acquires knowledge through reading, lecture, and study. Knowledge provides the conceptual foundation that informs and guides one's practice. *Skills*, or procedures, are the tools utilized. Every domain has specific procedures, often accompanied by sets of instructions, or rules, for their use. The learner studies the tools and observes the teacher or other role models apply them. Then the learner practices using the tools, ideally with feedback from the instructor. Finally, *attitudes* are the values and feelings toward the work and the people involved. These may be explicitly described during training; they are also implicit and observed by the learner. Sometimes the attitudes communicated nonverbally by role models are congruent with those taught formally, and sometimes they are discrepant.

It should be noted that sometimes people treat the terms skill and competency as synonyms. As Sperry (2010b) pointed out, there are similarities between skills and competencies, but there are also important differences. A skill is a capability, often acquired through training, but it does not include the knowledge or attitudinal components.

Here is an example of the three components in a domain very different from psychotherapy, that of the artist. Artists acquire knowledge of things like the rules of perspective and the color wheel, even if they actively choose to challenge those rules at times in their work. They learn specific skills, such as painting a watercolor wash, firing pottery, or

3

stretching a canvas. And they communicate an attitude in their work. It might be reverence for the subject and/or the medium, playfulness, satire, or many other things. Together, the components create a whole greater than the sum of its parts.

In psychotherapy as well, the three components do not operate independently of one another; rather, they are interrelated. Here is a psychotherapy example that illustrates the integration of the components. "Requesting feedback about how the therapy is going" is something done by highly effective therapists, discussed in much detail in this book. The highly effective therapist has the knowledge that client perceptions make a difference. He or she has the skills to elicit that information. In addition, he or she truly wants to know when things are not working well enough, so that they can be changed. This is very different from the request for feedback from the caricature of the service adviser from a car dealership, who may strongly encourage customers to give only superlative feedback. This exemplifies how attitude, not just the technique or the behavior, is an essential component of a competency.

ESSENTIAL CLINICAL COMPETENCIES

Each discipline has a somewhat different list of competencies, of course. And not all of the competencies of behavioral healthcare professionals involve psychotherapy (for example, psychiatrists prescribe medication; psychologists may conduct psychological testing). However, a cluster of competencies necessary for psychotherapy does emerge in multiple disciplines, with commonalities among the disciplines' lists.

Sperry (2010b) described six core competencies and twenty essential clinical competencies needed for highly effective therapy. These are not a random set of abilities. Just the opposite is the case, because they are highly interrelated. Table 1.1 lists these competencies.

Sperry (2010a) suggested that there are three main schools of psychotherapy practiced today: dynamic, cognitive, and systemic. In each of these approaches, the essential competencies are addressed in a different way. This book elaborates on how the 20 competencies emerge in highly effective systemic work in the solution-focused and strategic therapies.

4

Table 1.1   Core and Essential Clinical Competencies

Conceptual Foundation

Apply a conceptual map to understand and direct the therapeutic process

Relationship Building and Maintenance

Establish a positive relationship or effective therapeutic alliance

Assess readiness for change and foster treatment-promoting factors

Recognize and resolve resistance and ambivalence

Recognize and repair therapeutic alliance ruptures

Recognize and resolve transference and countertransference

Intervention Planning

Perform an integrative diagnostic assessment

Specify a *DSM* diagnosis

Develop an effective clinical case conceptualization

Develop an effective treatment plan

Draft an integrative clinical case report

Intervention Implementation

Establish a treatment focus

Maintain the treatment focus

Recognize and resolve treatment-interfering factors

Apply the specific interventions utilized in the approach

Intervention Evaluation and Termination

Monitor progress and modify treatment accordingly

Evaluate progress and prepare clients for termination

Culturally and Ethically Sensitive Practice

Develop an effective cultural formulation

Plan and implement tailored and culturally sensitive interventions

Make ethically sensitive decisions

Source: Highly Effective Therapy: Developing Essential Clinical Competencies in Counseling and Psychotherapy, by L. Sperry, 2010, New York, NY: Routledge, p. 8. Copyright 2010 by Taylor & Francis Group, LLC, a division of Informa plc. Adapted with permission of the publisher.

DEVELOPMENTAL STAGES OF COMPETENCY

As noted previously, a competency-based approach goes beyond minimal competency for practice. It includes an aspirational component, the striving toward excellence. From this perspective, there exist different levels of competency. One "stage model" was described by Dreyfus and Dreyfus (1986). A computer scientist and a philosopher, Dreyfus and Dreyfus combined their perspectives to propose a five-stage skill acquisition model, where people move from novice to expert by increasing the scope of perception and experience with the tasks required. Similar stages appear in skill acquisition research with airline pilots, chess players, drivers, and adult learners.

Dreyfus and Dreyfus's (1986) stages are as follows: *novice, advanced beginner, competent, proficient*, and *expert*. At each level, the learner becomes familiar with a skill by performing a set of activities. In the first stage, beginning learners follow basic rules, sometimes in a concrete way. They use little situational perception or discretionary judgment. The advanced beginner continues to follow rules but also begins to transfer rules to related situations. However, all rules may be treated equally, there may be limited ability to tailor to the specifics of the situation, and there is considerable reliance on a set of rules. At the third stage, that of competence, people can apply standard procedures in a variety of routine situations more independently. They demonstrate that they understand the relative importance of different rules. At the next stage, that of proficiency, decision making may be more automatic. The proficient person sees the whole based on extensive previous experience; he or she also perceives deviations from the usual pattern. Finally, the expert intuitively senses what needs to be done in a particular situation and which rules are most important in this specific case. As noted above, there is aspiration toward excellence, and becoming an expert is an ongoing journey, not a fixed destination.

BECOMING A MORE PROFICIENT PSYCHOTHERAPIST

How does one build proficiency as a therapist? Can expertise be taught? Atherton (2008) pointed out that most training is designed to bring the learner up to a level of competency (the third level, as described above) but that a critical question addresses what exactly it is that moves someone beyond competency to proficiency. Atherton asked:

What is the expertise which distinguishes a premier division footballer from the amateur who plays in the park, and whose idea of tactics is simply to chase the ball wherever it is? How does the skilled counselor form just the right question, in just the right tone, at just the right time, to enable a client to see her situation differently? How is the counselor able to take informed risks? How is that different from the well-meaning novice who is likely to miss the opportunity or unwittingly nudge her in an unproductive direction?

Sperry (2010b) asserted that one does not have to be a "born therapist" to achieve higher levels of proficiency. He suggested that competency can be enhanced through three types of learning: *declarative, procedural,* and *reflective.* Declarative learning builds knowledge and often grows through reading, study, discussion, and formal coursework. Procedural learning involves the application of knowledge and develops through clinical experience and supervision. Describing reflective learning, Rønnestad and Skovholt (2003) emphasized an attitude of continuous reflection and openness to new experience. People sometimes do this on their own, through thinking and/or writing. Sometimes reflective learning develops through consultation with colleagues or supervisors, and sometimes people continue to refine their practice through additional training. Usually they invite and incorporate feedback about the results of their work. However it is done, "reflective practice," as Schön (1983) described it, is thinking about what one is doing in order to learn from it.

It should be noted that although reflection appears to be one important component of expertise, it can also produce untested illusions of expertise (Atherton, 2008). Reflection may be necessary but not sufficient, something that should not be used alone. It may contribute to expertise; it may also occur as a result of it. Reflection appears to be most valuable when used in combination with supervision, consultation, and monitoring of outcomes. (Monitoring is discussed extensively in Chapter 8.)

Simply practicing therapy for a long time does not necessarily build proficiency. As Ericsson (2000) pointed out, once people reach a level of minimal competence, further improvement is not simply a function of years of experience. Therapists are quite capable of practicing at a minimal competency level for a very long time, and they may make the same error repeatedly. Those who achieve higher levels of proficiency tend to seek out what Ericsson called *deliberate practice.* Deliberate practice refers to activities designed to improve specific aspects of an ability. Advanced learners encode additional, more complex information; they also seem to

7

organize it in ways that allow them to adapt quickly to changing circumstances. They also monitor and evaluate their own performance, and they actively seek out and design new training experiences.

Atherton (2008) added three Cs to the stages beyond minimal competency: *contextualization, contingency*, and *creativity*. Contextualization refers to "when to do what." It involves discretion and discrimination, deciding which rule to apply. Contingency goes beyond predetermined recipes. It includes the flexibility to cope when things go wrong. There is strategic planning and thinking ahead, with anticipation of possibilities and ideas for dealing with them. Creativity involves using standard skills in new ways to solve new problems. Atherton noted that in a way the creativity component may be "… aspirational (but nevertheless recognisable [*sic*] when you get there)".

When an approach includes some nontraditional tools, is competency still relevant? The "rules" may be different at times in a nontraditional approach, but just because something is nontraditional does not mean that "anything goes." This is illustrated by an anecdote told about the 20th-century composer Hindemith, who wrote somewhat dissonant music. At a rehearsal, Hindemith said to the orchestra, "Gentlemen, gentlemen, even though it sounds wrong, it's still not right" (D. McNair, personal communication, Summer 2006).

COMPETENCIES IN SOLUTION-FOCUSED
AND STRATEGIC PRACTICE

This book addresses the specific knowledge, skills, and attitudes that comprise competency in the solution-focused and strategic therapies. It considers each of the six competencies and 20 clinical skills described by Sperry (2010b), elaborating on how each emerges in solution-focused and strategic work. In particular, it describes how solution-focused and strategic therapists can integrate knowledge, procedures, and attitude, aiming to move beyond minimal competence to the higher levels described in this chapter.

Chapter 2 reviews the background, theory, and methods of solution-focused therapy, brief strategic therapy, and an integrated strategic solution focused approach. It introduces the strategic notion that commonsense attempted solutions sometimes maintain or aggravate the problems they are supposed to be solving. It describes how identifying problems and interrupting unsuccessful attempted solutions became components of strategic therapy. Next, the chapter describes how solution-focused methods and attitudes evolved from strategic practice. It introduces the solution-focused perspective that pieces of the solution are usually already present. Solutions may seem unrelated to problems, and they can be discovered and amplified when the therapist "leads from behind." In the "doing what works" approach to solution-focused therapy, solution-focused methods and strategic ideas and tools are used together. *Clarifying problems, elaborating solutions, doing what works,* and *changing what does not* are recurring themes throughout this book.

Joining with the client is the first task of any therapy. Chapter 3 addresses how solution-focused and strategic therapists create relationships where the client feels safe, understood, and hopeful. It also covers how to assess readiness for change and foster treatment-promoting factors. There is discussion of how the therapist elicits the client's best hopes for treatment—and the "worst" thing a therapist could recommend! The chapter reviews ways of immediately discovering client strengths and resources, with clinical examples. When the therapist highlights client variables, things that often have nothing to do with the problem, the process simultaneously strengthens the therapeutic alliance and provides important clues about unique "ingredients of the solution." Clinical examples illustrate the process.

Chapter 4 covers how solution-focused and strategic therapists attempt to nurture therapeutic relationships that work for clients throughout treatment. It describes how to regularly check in with clients about how things are going in the work together, using both formal rating scales and ongoing discussion. Therapists are encouraged to ask questions such as "Are we where we should be?" and "What might we be doing differently?" Talking about these things openly, with fluctuating feelings, discomfort, and ambivalence viewed as normal rather than "deal breakers," is "doing what works" in the therapeutic relationship—and it provides practice for the client's relationships outside therapy as well. Case examples illustrate ways of addressing ruptures in the therapeutic alliance both by "going back to the basics" and by "doing something different."

Chapter 5 covers assessment at multiple levels. It considers multiaxial *Diagnostic and Statistical Manual of Mental Disorders* (DSM) diagnosis (American Psychiatric Association, 2000), cultural variables, readiness for change, and safety issues from solution-focused and strategic perspectives. The chapter addresses ways of viewing systemic issues, client strengths and resources, and the client's "theory of change." There is discussion of problem clarification, with focus on the highest priority concern and "why now." The chapter describes "best hopes inquiry" and solution elaboration as assessment tools, and it covers scaling questions. It reviews the assessment of "attempted solutions" and whether they are working well enough. "Exceptions," or "times when the problem isn't," are assessed in detail and highlighted, because amplifying these is a core component of solution-focused and strategic therapy.

In Chapter 6, there is discussion of how solution-focused and strategic therapists approach three of the core competencies that are part of a larger "intervention planning domain": clinical case conceptualization, treatment planning, and creating an integrative clinical case report. As discussed in previous chapters, the strategic solution focused therapist working with a new client has collected the following information: the client's view of the problem, the client's best hopes and worst fears, the client's readiness for change, the client's strengths, systemic variables, the client's view of a preferred future, pieces of the solution that are already happening, and solutions previously attempted both by the client and by others. Now it is time for the therapist to put all of this information together, in an integrative conceptualization of the case. From that case conceptualization will grow a treatment plan, tailored to this client's unique situation and designed to amplify what works and to change what does not. All of the above can then become part of a clinical report that captures the content and process of the interaction, simultaneously reflecting the attitudes of solution-focused and strategic therapy and providing documentation appropriate for the therapist's practice setting.

Chapter 7 covers the four competencies that are part of intervention implementation: establishing a treatment focus, maintaining the treatment focus, addressing treatment-interfering factors, and applying specific solution-focused and strategic procedures. It discusses how problem clarification and solution elaboration focus the work to the most important areas, and it addresses how highly competent therapists use variations of the basic tools to address obstacles when they arise. The chapter covers common unsuccessful attempted solutions in depression, anxiety, relationships, and longstanding personal patterns (personality disorders)—and some alternatives. There is discussion of how and when to incorporate didactic information, other methods, and other modalities into the process. The interventions selected are collaboratively tailored to the client's goals, needs, preferences, and style of learning, with emphasis on doing what works and the expectation that one size will not fit all.

Monitoring and evaluating clinical outcomes are covered in Chapter 8. Psychotherapy outcome research shows that change early in treatment and client ratings of the therapeutic alliance are associated with positive outcomes, so solution-focused and strategic therapists clearly want to know what is working. They also want to know when treatment is *not* working well enough, so that, in the spirit of the model, they can do something different. This chapter describes multiple ways in which solution-focused and strategic therapists routinely evaluate process and outcome. Sessions often begin with "What's better or different?" inquiry, which simultaneously monitors progress, highlights positive change, and guides the focus to areas of concern. Paper-and-pencil and computer-based rating scales that measure both symptoms and the relationship are sometimes used as well. Scaling questions, with endpoints anchored in the client's own language whenever possible, provide repeated measures of multiple variables, including progress, perception of significant others' views of progress, and confidence that change can be maintained.

Chapter 9 addresses the core competency involving evaluation of progress and preparation for termination in the strategic and solution-focused therapies. It discusses length of treatment—single session, brief, or intermittent—and covers how therapists and clients collaboratively make decisions about frequency of sessions and when to discontinue therapy. Sometimes the plan includes a "maintenance dose of psychotherapy," scheduled booster sessions, or an invitation to return if needed. Building on what works, the plan is tailored to individual client needs and influenced by progress toward goals, healthcare system variables (including insurance coverage and availability of appointments), and client preferences. Solution-focused conversations about a future that include "slips and recovery" and several strategic tools add a "relapse prediction and management" component to the work. The "doing what works and changing what doesn't" perspective, openly shared with clients, is a tool to use for maintenance of gains long after treatment has ended. As therapists and clients plan for termination, they review together both progress toward goals and feelings (often mixed) about the process. An acceptance-based component (that some discomfort, challenges, and patterns may continue to be present) may be balanced by a change-focused perspective that celebrates changes made, plans for continued growth, and previous success in getting back on track after slips.

Chapter 10 discusses how solution-focused and strategic therapists address the following two competencies: first, planning and implementing tailored and culturally sensitive interventions and, second, making ethically sensitive decisions. The therapist deliberately discovers, respects, and utilizes client variables in tailoring treatment to client needs, language, social resources, and preferences. The one-size-does-*not*-fit-all perspective can decrease well-intended but often erroneous assumptions that clients from similar ethnic, racial, or religious backgrounds will have the same symptoms and preferences. Case examples illustrate the process. Like therapists of any orientation, solution-focused and strategic therapists need to know and adhere to the ethical principles of their professions. Maintaining confidentiality, avoiding conflicts of interest, and other ethical issues are addressed in this chapter from the perspective of doing what works to respect the client's values, dignity, and rights. It is emphasized that doing what works emphatically does *not* mean that "any means justify the end." Just the opposite is true. When there is a paradoxical component to some strategic interventions (which sometimes predict the presence or recurrence of symptoms or patterns the client wishes to eliminate), the strategic solution focused therapist is transparent about the phenomenon. Therapists and clients discuss together the existential reality that symptoms and patterns do reappear and that anticipating and coping with them are often critical ingredients of the solution.

Chapter 11 describes optimal competency-based training that fosters highly effective practice beyond the minimum competency level; that is, at the proficient level of expertise and higher. It discusses how therapists at different stages of competency approach the knowledge, skills, and attitude components of the solution-focused and strategic therapies, with examples of different levels of competency. The chapter also describes some methods for moving to higher levels of competency. At the higher levels of solution-focused and strategic practice, therapists more quickly and intuitively recognize when something is not working for this client at this point in therapy. They listen carefully to their clients. They are flexible and creative, combining conceptual, procedural, and reflective information in new ways. The chapter introduces some specific solution-focused strategies that may be used in training programs, clinical supervision, and/or self-reflection, inviting therapists to embrace challenges, increase flexibility, and transform impasses into interactions that make a positive difference for each client today.

2

Understanding the Conceptual Basis of the Solution-Focused and Strategic Therapies

Just as a solid foundation provides the base for a strong building, a clear conceptual foundation is necessary for a psychotherapy approach. The conceptual foundation guides the therapist at every stage of the journey. Therapists may claim that they are eclectic and, as discussed throughout this book, therapists certainly integrate approaches—indeed, the very concept of strategic solution focused therapy represents such an integration. Sometimes (as in strategic solution focused therapy) the conceptual foundation is a deliberately blended or integrated approach. But whether it is "pure" or "integrated," therapists typically have a "default position" from which they work. They focus on some pieces of information and away from others. All other things being equal, they view clients, problems, goals, and the treatment process through the conceptual lens that guides them. Working chronologically, this chapter reviews the lenses used in brief strategic therapy, solution-focused therapy, and an integrated strategic solution focused model. It describes the background and theories of these approaches, and it briefly describes their methods, which are covered in more detail in later chapters. The chapter also introduces some core concepts, *clarifying problems, elaborating solutions, doing what works,* and *changing what does not,* which are recurring themes throughout this book.

BRIEF STRATEGIC THERAPY

Strategic therapy can be seen as an approach in which the therapist initiates what happens during therapy and develops a plan, or *strategy*, for the treatment. The strategic therapy emphasized in this book is primarily the model developed at the Mental Research Institute (MRI) Brief Therapy Center in Palo Alto, California. However, it should be pointed out that there are other systemic approaches that use strategic principles—and the term *strategic therapy*. All of them grew from the same conceptual foundation, an epistemology based on principles of systems and communication research and cybernetics. Ruesh and Bateson (1951) introduced these ideas into psychiatric thinking in the 1950s. In 1959, Don Jackson established the MRI in order to explore how these nontraditional ideas about interaction might be applied to psychiatric treatment. Jay Haley and Virginia Satir joined the movement, although they each eventually moved in slightly different directions. The models that grew from this foundation are often described as systemic therapies.

The variation of strategic therapy practiced by Jay Haley and his colleagues began to focus more on what happens at particular stages of the family life cycle. Haley's problem-solving strategic therapy emphasizes altering the social situation and sequence of interactions to produce change (Haley, 1973).

In another variation that emerged, the Milan systemic approach, Maria Selvini Palazzoli and her colleagues emphasized paradoxical prescriptions and circular and reflexive questioning. Using positive connotation, they attempted to create a climate where family members' intentions could be viewed as positive even in difficult situations (Boscolo, Cecchin, Hoffman, & Penn, 1987).

Another center of strategic practice, the Centro di Terapia Strategica of Arezzo, was founded by Giorgio Nardone and Paul Watzlawick in 1987. Therapists and applied researchers affiliated with this center have moved from general models of therapy to specific interventions for specific disorders. Nardone and Watzlawick (1993) described some of the disorder-specific protocols.

MRI BRIEF THERAPY: THEORY AND ASSUMPTIONS

In the book *Change: Principles of Problem Formation and Problem Resolution*, Paul Watzlawick, John Weakland, and Richard Fisch (1974) presented the principles on which brief strategic therapy is grounded. They differentiated between *difficulties,* defined as undesirable but common states of affairs that may resolve on their own or through simple adjustments or must simply be lived with, and *problems,* defined as impasses that are created and maintained by the mishandling of difficulties. They asserted that difficulties may be mishandled in three ways: First, action may be necessary but not taken, (e.g., someone may deny or ignore it when something is obviously wrong). Second, action may be taken when it should not be, as in an attempt to solve something that simply cannot be solved. Third, action may be taken at the wrong level. Examples here include trying to force spontaneity, seeking a no-risk method where risk is inevitable, trying to reach agreement by arguing, and attracting attention by trying to be left alone (Segal, 2001).

The MRI therapists also assumed that there are two ways things can change. In *first-order change,* change occurs *within* a system, with the system itself remaining unchanged. *Second-order change* alters the system. Here is an example for a common difficulty at any professional conference: complaints about the room temperature. A first-order response to the complaints involves turning the thermostat up or down every time someone complains. A second-order response to the anticipated difficulty occurs when the conference flier advises attendees: "Room temperatures are likely to fluctuate drastically. Please dress in layers."

It is emphasized that people do not mishandle difficulties "on purpose." They are not seeking "secondary gain." They genuinely believe that what they are doing is necessary and the most helpful thing to do. When attempts to solve the problem fail, this confirms that the problem is becoming severe or chronic. People therefore apply even more of the "logical" solution. These efforts work no better than they did the first time, and the original difficulty may even worsen. Problems are maintained inadvertently and often with the best of intentions. The core assumption is that

> ... the kind of problems people bring to psychotherapists PERSIST only if they are maintained by ongoing current behavior of the patient and others with whom he interacts. Correspondingly, if such problem-maintaining behavior is appropriately changed or eliminated, the problem will be resolved or vanish, regardless of its nature, origin, or duration. (Weakland, Fisch, Watzlawick, & Bodin, 1974, p. 144)

In the example above, the first-order response (adjusting the thermostat in response to every complaint) maintains the problem, because every time the room is warmer, someone else wants it cooler and vice versa. When the problem-maintaining response is replaced by the second-order approach, the problem might be resolved. These principles refer to changes within systems, and brief strategic therapy can be considered a systemic therapy.

The work of Milton Erickson, psychiatrist and hypnotist, also influenced the MRI therapists. Erickson often conducted hypnosis without inducing trance. He observed people closely and utilized their own words, styles, and body movements in his work with them. Sometimes he communicated in metaphor and used paradox. Erickson "seeded" ideas, building upon them later. He sometimes encouraged resistance and provided "worse" alternatives. Erickson also noticed the positive, sometimes relabeling or reframing a behavior or interaction in a more positive light. Using deviation amplification, Erickson discovered tiny changes and enlarged upon them (Haley, 1973). Erickson's influence is evident in many ways in all of the solution-focused and strategic therapies.

All of the concepts described above began to change the practice of therapy for the therapists at the MRI. At first the therapists began to apply the principles in their clinical practices on their own. Recalling how the Brief Therapy Project started, John Weakland said,

> Dick (Fisch) was doing therapy in his office and Paul (Watzlawick) was also excited about the possibility of getting together in a more formal way to do what we were doing anyway: talking about our difficult cases and seeing if we could look at them in a different way. (MRI.org, 2010)

Fisch founded the Brief Therapy Center in 1966.

MRI BRIEF STRATEGIC THERAPY: PROCEDURES

In the MRI Brief Therapy Project, cases were not screened, and clients could be seen up to 10 sessions. One therapist interviewed the client or family, and the others observed through a one-way mirror, phoning in suggestions during the session. The therapists used a four-step procedure (Watzlawick et al., 1974):

1. Clearly defining the problem in concrete terms
2. Investigating solutions attempted so far

3. Clearly defining the concrete change desired
4. Formulating and implementing a plan (or strategy) to produce that change

Often the strategy involved reframing. Suggestions or homework frequently aimed at replacing unsuccessful first-order attempted solutions with second-order alternatives. Sometimes the suggestions represented an intervention that might be seen as a "180-degree opposite" from the unsuccessful attempted solution. These procedures, described in more detail in Chapters 5, 6, and 7, remain the core tools in brief strategic therapy today.

Another important component of the MRI approach addressed motivating clients to implement new behaviors. The therapists assessed who in a family (or other social system) was the primary *customer* for change. Recognizing that people are often quite reluctant to discontinue behaviors that may seem to be "the only thing one can do," they also carefully considered what they called *position*. Position referred to the client's attitudes and beliefs about the problem, its origin, and what it would take to solve it, and it was influenced by cultural and occupational variables. This sensitivity to cultural variables is elaborated in Chapter 10. Interventions were presented in a manner consistent with position variables.

ATTITUDES IN BRIEF STRATEGIC THERAPY

As described in Chapter 1, *attitude* is an integral part of any therapeutic approach. At MRI, there was an absolute refusal to pathologize people for their complaints. Psychiatric diagnosis was not considered to be necessary or helpful, and there was a belief that diagnostic labeling might actually detract from what was most important: what a person does in a specific social context and how others react to that. This was the case even when behaviors might be influenced by or associated with some biological factors. One did not need to review or understand the past in order to solve the problem now. Therapy should be brief: "Lest therapy become its own pathology, it must limit itself to the relief of suffering; the quest for happiness cannot be its task" (Watzlawick et al., 1974, p. 57).

The brief strategic therapists asserted that all therapists influence their clients. They valued being open and explicit about that process and talked about using influence deliberately and responsibly. There was a willingness to be direct, to suggest the unexpected, and to use paradox toward the

17

end of achieving the goal. The change suggested might be small and seemingly insignificant, but its effects might be far reaching. The MRI therapists recognized that a tiny change can produce larger changes in a system.

Another attitude involved the importance of therapist *maneuverability*. There was a sense that the therapist needs to keep options open throughout treatment, shifting as needed. Shifting stances is an important skill at the higher levels of competency. A related concept is that of *one-downsmanship*. Brief strategic therapists tend to take a low-keyed, conversational stance. This may function to put clients at ease and becomes part of the therapeutic alliance. This concept is discussed in more detail in Chapters 3 and 4.

SOLUTION-FOCUSED THERAPY

Solution-focused methods and attitudes evolved from strategic practice. Steve de Shazer and Insoo Kim Berg trained at MRI and established the Brief Family Therapy Center (BFTC) in Milwaukee in the 1980s. Noticing that problems, even severe ones, do not happen all the time, they focused more closely on the problem-absent times, which they called *exceptions*. Working from the same deviation-amplifying assumptions that Erickson and the MRI therapists utilized, de Shazer and his colleagues worked to amplify solution sequences. They developed the "First Session Task," which asked clients to do the following: "Between now and the next time we meet, I want you to observe so you can describe to me next time what happens in your (life, family, marriage, relationship) that you want to continue to have happen" (de Shazer, 1985, p. 137). The BFTC therapists increasingly saw that people already have the resources to solve problems and in fact may have already done so. Solutions were already in clients' behavioral repertoires.

Like the MRI therapists, the BFTC therapists often worked with couples and families. They believed that solutions are interactional, often involving other people. They recognized that one tiny change leads to another, and then another, and that the changes that follow lead to changes in other members of the family or social system. Thus, like brief strategic therapy, solution-focused therapy can be considered a systemic therapy (de Shazer & Dolan, 2007).

de Shazer was an avid student of Wittgenstein's philosophy, which emphasizes the concept of "facts" or things within their surroundings or context. Things are considered to be meaningful only within the context of the whole. According to this philosophy, language, too, can only be understood in its home context, and when it is removed from that context, its meaning is easily lost. As cited in de Shazer and Dolan (2007), Wittgenstein asserted that

> … pictures of facts are mirrored in language to give us meaning, so that we can clearly say that a hippopotamus is not in the room. Of course, a fact can always be otherwise. We can imagine a hippo in a room. (p. 109)

Like the brief strategic therapists, the solution-focused therapists also assumed that therapists influence their clients. de Shazer focused carefully on the client's language, in the client's context, and on how the therapist's language shapes client responses. This interest influenced the development of solution-focused therapy, eventually leading to collaboration between linguistics/communication researchers and solution-focused therapists on macroanalysis process research. Solution-focused therapists value the creative, active use of language in a "coconstructive" process (De Jong and Bavelas, 2010).

The BFTC therapists also began to notice that clients' solutions were often unrelated to the problem. Describing this phenomenon in an interview with Victor Yalom, Berg said:

> We discovered that there's no connection between a problem and its solution. No connection whatsoever. Because when you ask a client about their problem, they will tell you a certain kind of description, but when you ask them about their solutions, they give you entirely different descriptions of what the solution would look like for them. So a horrible alcoholic family will say, "We will have dinner together and talk together. We will go for a walk together." (Berg, as cited in Yalom & Rubin, 2010, Solution-Focused Model section)

For the BFTC therapists, clear definition of the problem and the attempted solution—core procedures in the MRI approach—were not seen as necessary. Interrupting unsuccessful solutions was no longer the therapist's primary focus. Instead, the therapist's task was to create opportunities for clients to apply their own solutions. As clients did so, they would view themselves as more competent and resourceful (Metcalf, 2001).

19

SOLUTION-FOCUSED PROCEDURES:
FUTURE-FOCUSED INQUIRY

Berg, de Shazer, and their colleagues did want clients to define their goals, clearly, specifically, and in small, achievable steps. In this respect, they were similar to the MRI team. They were interested in knowing how clients wanted their lives to be. This led to the development of the miracle question. In an interview with Hayes (1991), Berg described how the miracle question emerged "by accident." The story goes like this: On the way into the therapy room, a client was telling Berg how serious her problems were. In this context, the client said, "It would take a miracle to solve my problem," and Berg decided to find out what the client meant by that.

Miracle questions invite description of a preferred future, with elaboration of specific detail. Clients are encouraged to notice pieces of their miracles that are already happening (the exceptions) and to build on them. The miracle question and its variations are described in more detail in Chapters 5, 6, and 7. Tailoring miracle questions to specific client stances and cultural variables is an important skill at the higher levels of proficiency in solution-focused and strategic solution focused therapy, addressed throughout this book.

Another solution-focused tool is *scaling*. Scaling questions ask clients to rate their progress toward various goals, and they have both assessment and intervention functions. The coping question, another solution-focused procedure, is one variation of a miracle question. Coping questions are used when clients do not perceive progress toward the goal or in other difficult situations. These tools can be used at multiple levels of proficiency and are covered in later chapters.

As at MRI, the BFTC therapists often worked in front of the one-way mirror, with input from colleagues. Often the therapist and client took a "break" for team discussion of end-of-session input. In settings where there is not the luxury of a treatment team and time for a break, some solution-focused therapists take a few minutes near the end of a session to leave the room briefly, to collect their thoughts about any feedback to be given, or they may pause without leaving the room. The feedback often compliments clients on things they are doing that are working. It may suggest experiments or other ways of building on solutions that are already present or discovering new ones.

ATTITUDES IN SOLUTION-FOCUSED THERAPY

Like brief strategic therapists, solution-focused therapists do not focus extensively on the past, pathology, or formal psychiatric diagnosis. They do not assume that clients need to "work through" old conflicts in order to create change in the present and the future, and they agree that therapy does not need to go on for a long period of time. However, unlike brief strategic therapists, who emphasize the importance of clarifying the problem, solution-focused therapists do not think that much problem clarification is necessary. Although highly proficient solution-focused therapists respect clients' desires to talk about problems at times (a topic discussed later in this book), the solution-focused attitude conveys far more interest in solution building than in problem solving.

Solution-focused therapists value careful listening to the client. As already discussed, there is an assumption that the client already has the strengths and resources within to resolve the problem. There is an expectation that attentive listening, or being a "solution detective," can provide "clues" toward the solution. This attitude is reflected in the title of de Shazer's 1988 book: *Clues: Investigating Solutions in Brief Therapy*. The assumption is that the client, not the therapist, is the true expert on this situation.

To discover the clues that will lead the way toward the goal (which has been set by the client), solution-focused therapists "lead from behind" (de Shazer & Dolan, 2007). Taking a collegial, conversational stance, they tend to ask more questions and make fewer declarative statements, and they rarely, if ever, make interpretations or confrontational statements. Homework ideas are not "assigned" by an "expert." They may come from the client or they may be cocreated.

Solution-focused therapy conveys an attitude of respect, where clients are valued and supported. Berg frequently said "Wow!" in response to some client statements. That exclamation expresses the flavor of solution-focused admiration, often mixed with surprise and excitement, about some client verbalization or behavior.

STRATEGIC SOLUTION FOCUSED THERAPY

The strategic solution focused perspective blends the strategic and solution-focused principles, procedures, and attitudes described above. Also referred to as "the doing what works approach to solution-focused therapy" (Quick, 2010b), this model emerged in the early 1990s. This author was a member of an informal peer supervision group in San Diego, which later described itself as the Strategic Solution Focused Interest Group.[1] The members of this group were all practicing brief strategic therapy, although some of them also included cognitive behavioral, existential, and Gestalt therapy; psychoeducation; and hypnosis in their work. These therapists began to learn about the solution-focused approach. They were excited by the new ideas about building on already-existing solutions and leading from behind, and they saw the powerful change that resulted when they applied these ideas.

At the same time, they recognized that there were some parts of the strategic model that they valued and wanted to retain. They puzzled over this dilemma. Solution building was powerful, yet there still seemed to be times when a suggestion to interrupt an unsuccessful attempted solution made a tremendous positive difference. They also wondered: Was it possible to be solution-focused and still find value in problem clarification?

Then, in true solution-focused spirit, someone asked this question: What if using strategic therapy and solution-focused therapy together was not a problem any more? What might that look like? What if combining the theories, tools, and attitudes not only was not a *problem* but actually an emerging *solution*? From the questions of dilemma grew the beginnings of the integrated approach.

STRATEGIC SOLUTION FOCUSED THERAPY: THEORY

In the planned integration, the theory and techniques of brief *strategic* therapy are summarized as follows: Problems are often maintained by attempted solutions. Therefore, the therapist needs to clarify the problem and the attempted solution. If the solution is unsuccessful and/or maintaining the problem, the therapist should facilitate interruption of that attempted solution.

Solution-focused therapy is summarized in this way: Small pieces of the solution are already present and can grow into larger solutions. The therapist's tasks are to elicit and elaborate solutions and to facilitate building on them.

In the integrated *strategic solution focused*[2] approach, there is a "three-part theory" (Quick, 2008, p. 2):

1. What's the trouble? ("If it's not broken, don't fix it.")
2. If it works, do more of it.
3. If it doesn't work, stop doing it. Do something different.

As stated in *Doing What Works in Brief Therapy*, "in the combined model, problem clarification complements and enhances solution elaboration, while amplification of successful solutions complements and enhances interruption of unsuccessful solutions" (Quick, 2008, p. 10). The theory and tools are not new: "What is different here is that the procedures are deliberately used together" (Quick, p. 11). The combined approach is shown below:

Contributions of Brief Strategic Therapy and Solution-Focused Therapy to the Strategic Solution Focused Approach

Brief Strategic Therapy		Solution-Focused Therapy
Problem clarification	+	Solution elaboration
	and	
Interruption of what does not work	+	Amplification of what works

In addition, the principles operate at multiple levels:

(T)he critical elements in strategic solution focused therapy operate at two levels simultaneously. Working with the client, the therapist attempts to clarify the problem and to facilitate the client's doing what works and changing what does not. At the same time, the therapist selects techniques tailored to each situation, shifting to something different in response to problems or obstacles as they arise. (Quick, 2008, p. xviii)

There is an additional level as well. Identifying the area for change, doing what works, and changing what does not become the components of a *philosophy* shared with clients. Strategic solution focused therapists actively invite clients to apply the "doing what works principles" on their own as well as in psychotherapy.

PROCEDURES IN STRATEGIC SOLUTION FOCUSED THERAPY

There are four main tasks in strategic solution focused therapy: clarifying problems, elaborating solutions, identifying and evaluating attempted solutions, and planning and providing three-part feedback. This feedback is designed to build on what works and to change what does not. Later chapters describe all of these procedures in more detail, with discussion and examples of how they are applied at different levels of proficiency. The following outline summarizes the steps in strategic solution focused therapy.

STRATEGIC SOLUTION FOCUSED THERAPY OUTLINE[3]

1. Problem clarification
   a. *What's the trouble?* (you're here about today/you're hoping I can help you with)
   b. Definition of *highest-priority* problem. *In what way* is it a problem? Why *now*?
   c. What is your hope about *how* I will help?
   d. What's the *worst* message I could be giving you today? The *best* or most helpful message?
2. Solution elaboration
   a. *Miracle question:* You wake up tomorrow and the problem you're here about is solved. What will be different? What else? What will (person in your life) notice about you? How will he (she) be different? What else will be different as a result of these changes? What else? What else?
   b. *Exceptions:* Are there "pieces of the solution" that are already happening? How did you do that?!
   c. Scaling questions:
      Progress: On a scale from 0 to 10, where 0 is when the problem was at its worst and 10 is when it is resolved to your satisfaction, where are you now? (x = client's response)
      – How did you do that?!
      – How did you get to x?
      – First sign of change: How will you know you're at $x + 1$?
3. Assessment of attempted solutions
   a. What have you tried? How did you do that? Exactly what did you say?
   b. Did it work?
4. Feedback
   Would you like some feedback? (if yes):

a. Validate chief complaint—for example, "I don't blame you for feeling distressed …"
b. Compliment—for example, "I'm impressed that even in the face of … you've been able to …"
c. Suggestion/input:
   If what you're doing works,
   – Do more of it!
   – Pay attention to *how* you do it.
   If what you're doing doesn't work,
   – Stop doing it!
   – Do something different!
   – Pay attention to how you "turn the problem up and down."
   – Pay attention to how you cope with the problem.
   – Therapist formulates an alternate response that would, if performed, interrupt unsuccessful attempted solution.
   – Therapist presents the alternative in language/context client is most tlikely to hear.
5. What do you most want to remember from our conversation today?
6. Plan for additional service
   a. "Where shall we go from here? Do you want to make another appointment with me?" If yes, "When?" (No predetermined number of appointments or standard interval between appointments assumed.) "Or should we leave it open-ended?" (Family practice/intermittent care model)
   b. Referral/plan for other service (medication consult, group, class, feedback to other provider, etc.) as indicated.

ATTITUDES IN STRATEGIC SOLUTION FOCUSED THERAPY

Strategic solution focused therapy blends brief strategic therapy and solution-focused therapy *attitudes* as well as their theories and techniques. There is a focus on the present and the future more than on the past or on pathology. Therapy is generally brief. Small changes are expected to lead to bigger ones. Clients are valued, supported, and respected. They are considered to be the experts on their lives, on identifying what they

25

want to change, and on what works for them. There is an expectation that solutions have already begun to happen and that they sometimes appear in unexpected places. Clients are viewed as competent and able to learn and apply the *doing what works philosophy*, as well as other psychoeducational information that may be shared at times during therapy.

In the blended model, ambivalence is considered normal and is openly discussed—and acknowledged and modeled by the therapist, where appropriate. There is also an attitude that both "bumps on the road of life" and "slips and recovery" are normal phenomena. There is an expectation that people are resilient and have the resources to get through difficulty and create important changes (Quick, 2008).

Flexibility is valued in the strategic solution focused approach. There is an expectation that different things will work for different people—and for the same person at different times. Individual paths to solution are expected, so strategic solution focused therapy is tailored to individual variables. These include cultural considerations and are elaborated in Chapter 10. There is openness to surprise and discovery, with the idea that solutions sometimes appear in unexpected places. One size definitely does not fit all in this model!

THE CLASSICS AND THE HYBRIDS

The MRI and BFTC models have influenced therapists around the world, and their tools have been applied in many settings. It is evident from this chapter that there is diversity within the community of the solution-focused and strategic therapies. One might say that this community includes both "classics" and "hybrids." The classics follow the principles of either strategic therapy or solution-focused therapy essentially as they were originally developed, using a relatively "pure" model. In addition to the strategic solution focused therapy model described in this chapter, there are other variations that can be considered to be hybrids. Using different imagery, Avard (2010) compared solution-focused therapy to watercolors. He noted that some therapists add richness and variety to their work by adding new "colors" to the "paint box," while others advocate using as few "colors" as possible and "combin[ing] them in many, many ways" (p. 238). He noted that he is in the latter category.

Some therapists in the both the solution-focused community and in the strategic therapy community might say that tools from different approaches should *not* be combined, whereas others support combining what works. As discussed at the European Brief Therapy Association 2010 conference (Quick, 2010a), there is room for both classics and hybrids in the international therapist community, with emerging applications and continuing dialogue.

THE CONCEPTUAL FOUNDATION AND STAGES OF PROFICIENCY

How do therapists understand and use the conceptual foundation of the solution-focused and strategic therapies at each of the levels of proficiency described in Chapter 1? At the beginner stage, therapists may just be starting to learn about brief strategic therapy, solution-focused therapy, or the combined approach. There may be solid grounding in another approach, with a little knowledge of a few strategic or solution-focused techniques (perhaps from brief exposure at a workshop or from reading an article). Therapists at this stage may apply a particular technique, especially with consultation or supervision, but they are unlikely to fully understand, appreciate, or apply the skills or convey the attitudes of the solution-focused and strategic therapies.

Advanced beginners know more about the conceptual foundation. They could probably "pass an exam" (at the graduate school level) on the basics. They may be able to accurately describe how brief strategic therapy differs from solution-focused therapy and how the integrated approach combines the two. With supervision or consultation, they may be able to use the basic tools and convey the central attitudes.

At the level of minimum competency, solution-focused and strategic therapists probably know the basic history, tools, and attitudes of their approach and can describe it without "just having read about it." They can describe their orientation to an interested colleague, a trainee, or a supervisor. They can use the tools and communicate the attitudes in routine situations. In supervision or case conferences, they can usually identify which part of the model they are using.

Highly proficient solution-focused and strategic therapists know the conceptual foundation at a deeper level. They probably have read and discussed the primary sources multiple times. They may enjoy returning to that literature occasionally, and they may enjoy watching videos of sessions conducted by those who developed the approaches. They watch such videos with "new eyes," seeing nuances that may not have been apparent initially. They may keep up with the literature in the field, and they may teach the approach to trainees. Most important, they think about the conceptual foundation and consider how it emerges in what they are doing, especially in complicated situations. This does not have to be a daily occurrence—and, in the lives of most busy practitioners, it probably is not—but it is a knowledge that is always there, "in one's bones," and it can be articulated.

As described in the previous chapter, being an expert is aspirational, a journey rather than a destination, and it is continuous with the process described above. At the expert level, solution-focused and strategic therapists are likely to reflect on how to apply theory and attitude in their practices. In addition, one might argue that they contribute to the evolution of the conceptual foundation by learning from what emerges in the therapy they conduct—what works and what does not—to further fine-tune and develop concepts, techniques, and applications in new and creative ways.

NOTES

1. Linda Brown, Nancy Haller, Robert Mashman, Lisa Peterson, Marian Richetta, and Mark Schlissel were core members of this group.
2. Because *strategic solution focused* is not hyphenated in other books and articles on the approach, that convention is continued in this book. In other contexts, *solution-focused* is hyphenated.
3. From *Doing What Works in Brief Therapy: A Strategic Solution Focused Approach* (2nd ed., pp. 12–13), by E. Quick, 2008, San Diego, CA: Elsevier. Copyright 2008 by Elsevier. Adapted with permission of the publisher.

3

Forming an Effective Therapeutic Alliance

Joining with the client is the first task of any therapy. This chapter discusses two of the essential competencies in the domain of relationship building and maintenance. First, it addresses how strategic, solution-focused, and strategic solution focused therapists create therapeutic relationships where clients feel safe, understood, and hopeful. Second, it covers how to assess readiness for change and foster treatment-promoting factors. There is discussion of how to immediately discover client strengths and resources. When the therapist highlights client variables, things that often have nothing to do with the problem, the process simultaneously strengthens the therapeutic alliance and provides important clues about unique "ingredients of the solution." The chapter also introduces how the therapist elicits the client's best hopes for treatment—and the "worst" thing a therapist could recommend. Clinical examples illustrate the process.

COMMON FACTORS IN PSYCHOTHERAPY

As readers of this book probably know, evidence-based treatment is an actively discussed topic in the contemporary psychotherapy world, with much lively discussion about "what counts" as evidence-based treatment. In the "common factors vs. specific techniques" debate, one group of researchers has emphasized that specific treatments work for specific conditions. Other authors have focused on research that comes from meta-analyses of psychotherapy outcome research. Lambert (1992) wrote that 40% of the variance could be accounted for by what he called *client factors*. Motivation, relationships, demographic characteristics, resources, and events in clients' lives that occur outside of therapy fall into this category. *Relationship variables* account for 30% of the variance. This is the therapist–client bond or the therapeutic alliance. *Expectancy for change* accounts for another 15%. This component includes hope. *Specific techniques*, or the model, account for 15% of the variance. As Quick (2008) pointed out, this is far less than many therapists might anticipate.

Norcross (2005) described the common factors as transtheoretical, relevant in all models of therapy, and he asserted that all therapists, regardless of orientation, can use these variables to create conditions that facilitate change. Therapists of different orientations do so in different ways, but they all establish relationships, and they all do *something* to provide a change-promoting environment. This is the competency covered in this chapter.

Bohart and Tallman (2010) discussed the variable that accounts for the greatest proportion of the variance, client factors. They pointed out that client factors might include persistence or a supportive grandmother and that these factors can be unpredictable, emerging one client at a time and one alliance at a time. Duncan (2010) agreed that identifying and tailoring treatment to these variables is critical in successful therapy. He wrote, "If we don't recruit those idiosyncratic contributions ... we are doomed to fail" (p. 21).

Duncan also addressed the contribution of the model in combination with the *therapist's* expectancy of positive change. On one level, the model (the specific techniques component) only accounts for 15% of the variance. However, far more important than the model, Duncan said, is "the model delivered." The model delivered includes multiple components. In addition to the model's specific methods and theories, there is the therapist's allegiance to the model. The therapist believes in the client's capacity for change and healing as a result of using certain procedures. This belief is communicated, and this can contribute to the client's beliefs about change, adding an additional healing dimension. This therapist belief in the approach is part of the attitudinal component emphasized in this book.

Describing this phenomenon from a related perspective, Wampold (2007) noted that even when therapists are selected for their skill with a technique, the therapist effect is greater than differences among treatments. He hypothesized that this may be related to the fact that some therapists have the ability to form working alliances with a wide variety of clients. Again, *how* a treatment is delivered may be the crucial variable. When the therapist is trusted, that therapist's clients may work more collaboratively to achieve their goals. Duncan (2010) added that those clinicians who get the best results regularly seek feedback about two things: progress toward the goal and client perception of the therapeutic alliance. Ways of doing this are described in more detail in Chapters 4 and 8.

THE THERAPEUTIC ALLIANCE: AN ESSENTIAL INGREDIENT IN THE SOLUTION

As discussed above, the relationship between therapist and client is a critical component of psychotherapy throughout the course of treatment, significantly impacting both process and outcome. Bordin (1979) gave a classical definition of the therapeutic alliance. There are three elements: (a) the relational bond between therapist and client—the client's perception of therapist warmth, empathy, and genuineness; (b) agreement on the goals of treatment; and (c) agreement on the tasks and details of treatment. Sperry (2010a) described this as a meeting of the hearts and the minds. He elaborated by noting that when the meeting of the hearts is successful, a bond is established. As a result, the client feels understood, safe, and hopeful. The meeting of the minds refers to Bordin's second and third elements, and it includes a shared understanding of the methods to be used (both during sessions and outside therapy).

The therapeutic alliance is an ever-shifting process. If there is contact between the therapist and the client before the first session (for example, during a telephone contact), the relationship begins then. The first session creates first impressions and is therefore tremendously important (for better or for worse), and what the therapist does during an initial visit can set the tone for an entire course of therapy. Every contact, in person, by phone, e-mail, or letter, influences the relationship. Both therapist and client contribute to the process, which develops over time. Therapeutic alliances can be resilient and recover from rifts, a topic covered in more detail in the next chapter.

READINESS FOR CHANGE: VISITOR, COMPLAINANT, AND CUSTOMER

An integral part of attunement to the client involves recognizing his or her readiness to change and matching the therapist's stance to the client's. Prochaska and DiClemente (1992) have described stages that people go through in preparation for change. This process occurs with both issues that people bring to therapy and everyday decisions (such as changing one's hairstyle or buying a new cell phone). The first stage is *precontemplation*, where the person is not considering change at all (even though others may be suggesting it). In the *contemplation* stage, one is considering the change. People often remain in this stage for a long period of time, and sometimes they experience relief upon learning that this is quite common. *Preparation* follows: This is the time when the person is actively collecting information about the change and is planning to make the change soon. In the *action* stage, change is implemented, and in the *maintenance* stage, it is maintained. Often multiple attempts to change occur before a change is made. It is sometimes useful to describe these stages, emphasizing their universality and the normalcy of long periods of contemplation and multiple change attempts prior to success.

Solution-focused and strategic therapies have a similar framework. They consider the different stances a client may take, using the categories of *customer*, *complainant*, and *visitor*. Some ways of assessing readiness for change are discussed in Chapter 5. Specific therapist stances accompany each of the three client possibilities. The client who is a customer is in the action stage, ready to implement change. Thinking systemically, the therapist attempts to identify which member of a family or system is the customer—and "for what." This is done through careful listening and inquiry. When the client is a customer, suggestions or experiments to take action may be more likely to succeed.

Complainants are not yet ready to take action. They may very much want some other member of the family or larger system to change, but in regard to changing their own behavior, they may be in the stages of preparation or contemplation. Accurate recognition of this stance cautions the therapist not to rush into suggesting action that the person may not be ready to take. Instead, the therapist may invite observation, including observation of clues that will let one know that readiness to change is shifting. Permission for (or education about) the normalcy of ambivalence sometimes occurs at this stage.

32

Visitors have often come to therapy at the request of someone else. Sometimes this is obvious, as in the case when treatment is mandated, but people who appear to be self-referred are sometimes visitors too. Careful inquiry about what led up to the appointment—that is, why the person is here *now*—sometimes reveals that a family member (who may not be in the room) or someone else in the system is the true customer. As described by Quick (2008), one treats a visitor as one would treat a visitor to one's home. As a gracious host, one thanks the visitor for coming and invites him or her to return if desired.

Customer, complainant, and visitor stances change during therapy. Visitors become complainants and customers—sometimes for something other than that for which they were referred. Complainants notice new things, both in the outside world and within, and they become customers. A customer's motivation may decline, or he or she may discover the normal reluctance that accompanies so many changes.

As competency in recognizing and shifting stances grows, solution-focused and strategic therapists expect these shifts, and they are better able to track and recognize them as they occur. Because they are attuned to the shifts, they can respond to them more quickly. At the lower levels of proficiency, a therapist may assume that a client who appeared to be a customer at the first session will always welcome change-focused homework. Or he or she may "write off" a visitor as uninterested in or incapable of change. An attitudinal component here is nonjudgmental acceptance of any stage (as opposed to an implicit—or explicit—message that communicates something like this: "If you are coming to me for therapy, I expect you to be a customer, and if you aren't, that's an undesirable thing").

THE THERAPEUTIC ALLIANCE IN
BRIEF STRATEGIC THERAPY

As discussed previously, in brief strategic therapy there is a refusal to pathologize, regardless of the nature of any presenting complaint. From the very beginning, the therapist displays interest in viewing the problem as the complainant sees it, with careful listening and attention to detail. The therapist assumes that the client must have good reasons for any behavior or feeling, and he or she communicates a sincere desire to understand these things. The therapist's "default position" is one of believing the client: "It makes sense that you feel the way you do, in view of what you've experienced." This is an attitudinal component, conveyed through the kind of inquiry conducted.

In addition, therapists use particular methods to decrease any implied distance between the client and the therapist. Segal (2001) described some of the ways in which strategic therapists attempt to put clients at ease. First, the therapist is typically low key and conversational. Second, he or she may suggest that everyone use first names. "Rather than seeming to be a person with no problems and total understanding, the therapist portrays himself as another human being with frailties and limitations of his own" (p. 90).

Fisch and Schlanger (1999) noted that brief strategic therapists may use humor. They emphasized that this must be done carefully, but it can be beneficial. Empathic humor and references to universal human dilemmas can transform pathology to a familiar, shared context. This can normalize and become healing.

Brief strategic therapists may use what has been called the "Columbo approach." Columbo was a scruffy-looking Los Angeles detective in a rumpled raincoat in an American television series. He looked absent-minded but had an amazing eye for detail and a dedication that resulted in his solving all his cases. As R. Fisch (personal communication, Fall, 1991) pointed out, it is quite easy for therapists, in their desire to seem empathic and astute, to nod, say, "Uh-huh," and act "as if" they understand—when they really do not. Fisch emphasized that this does not help the client in the long run and that it is far more helpful to convey caring by saying, "No, I *don't* understand yet, so please help me to do so."

The therapeutic alliance has not been discussed as much in the literature on brief strategic therapy as in the literature on many other treatment approaches. However, it has always been an integral part of the process. Kleckner, Frank, Bland, and Amendt (1992) wrote:

> We would like to suggest that one of strategic therapy's best kept secrets is its utilization of client feelings in the treatment process. It's not that strategic therapists don't deal with feelings—it's just that they don't talk about it with each other, write about it in the literature, or teach it to trainees. ... Strategic therapists use feelings to help clients reach their goals, rather than focus on them as the main component of therapy. (p. 49)

It should be noted that this book changes the absence of discussion of the relationship in brief strategic therapy. It does so by explicitly stating that creating and maintaining the therapeutic alliance is one of the competencies in brief strategic therapy and by describing the knowledge, attitudes, and procedures that have been present all along.

Fisch and Schlanger (1999) gave an example of an alliance-building empathic statement in a portion of an interview conducted by Weakland. After a description of some difficult times, the therapist says, "It must be exhausting for you" (Weakland, as cited in Fisch & Schlanger, 1999, p. 49). Empathy with client discouragement builds the relationship and simultaneously sets the stage for a message to "take your time" that will be provided later in the therapy.

Brief strategic therapists emphasize the importance of maintaining maneuverability. Joining with the client, like everything else in treatment, is tailored to individual styles. Sometimes the very first contact interrupts a commonsense approach to relationship building, if there is a reason to believe that the typical approach could be maintaining the problem. Fisch and Schlanger (1999) gave an example of this at a high level of proficiency.

The client, Jerry,[1] a man in his 20s, referred by his minister, was anxious because he was sure that the FBI had him under surveillance. His minister accompanied him to his appointment and, at Jerry's request, into the therapist's office. As the therapist (Fisch) began the session, Jerry interrupted to ask whether Fisch could show him some identification.

R. F.: Sure; what do you want to see?

Jerry: How about your driver's license?

R. F.: OK. *(I get up from my chair, walk over to Jerry, and open my wallet to show him the license. He takes a quick glimpse of it, and I return to my chair.)*

Jerry: Thank you. That's OK.

R. F.: Are you satisfied I am who I'm supposed to be: Dr. Fisch?

Jerry: Yes.

R. F.: Man! You hardly looked at it; just a quick glance. You can't tell just from that. Here, take a good look at it. *(I go over to him again, showing him my license. This time, he looks at it carefully, studying the picture, glancing up at me to check it, and looking at it again.)*

Jerry: All right. It's OK.

R. F.: *(I return to my seat.)* You're satisfied now?

Jerry: Yeah, it's fine.

R. F.: God! Your minister told me on the phone that you're in a sweat about the FBI following you around, and you just accept that I'm OK from a simple driver's license?!

Jerry: Well, you've got those diplomas and your license on the wall.

R. F.: Jerry, it's nothing for the FBI to make up any kind of document. They could even outfit a whole office in no time at all. No; that won't do. I don't want you telling me anything about yourself until I'm convinced you're sure I'm who I'm supposed to be.

> A long silence ensued as Jerry desperately looked around the office for some corroborating item. Once or twice, he looked over to his minister, apparently in hope he would get him off the hook or suggest something he himself had overlooked. Finally, Jerry said, "Dr. Fisch, forget the FBI. That's not why I'm here. My wife is threatening to divorce me; I'm in a panic. Please, I need help with that." (Fisch & Schlanger, 1999, pp. 34–35)[2]

This excerpt illustrates a way of joining with the client that was definitely nontraditional. Taken outside the context of the theory and the details of the situation, it may seem bizarre or disrespectful. However, it was not a random or disrespectful choice. Rather, it grew from the therapist's rapid attunement to the client's initial response, in combination with his knowledge, skills, and attitude. The client's response, which clearly identified the precipitant to his immediate panic, showed that the therapist had succeeded in joining with the client and creating conditions favorable to treatment.

THE THERAPEUTIC ALLIANCE IN
SOLUTION-FOCUSED THERAPY

In solution-focused therapy, the therapeutic alliance is enhanced by the therapist's interest in the person and his or her life, strengths, and previous solutions. There is an expectation that clients are resilient, with a desire to work together to expand client options. A critical skill is the ability to listen, along with the attitude of truly wanting to listen and building on what is heard. As Dolan (2009) said, "You don't just *want* the client's response; you are *absolutely dependent* on it." In a conversation about "advanced solution-focused listening," she encouraged therapists to discover their own unique ways to listen and elicit personal detail. Through listening, the solution-focused therapist takes time early in the session to find out how the client spends the day and what he or she is good at. de Shazer said, "Any solution has to fit into the client's everyday life. Otherwise, it will, of course, be rejected. So we need at least some details of this everyday life" (de Shazer & Dolan, 2007, p. 74).

One part of listening involves not rushing in too quickly when the client does not immediately answer a question. This conveys: "I believe that you have an answer to the question I just asked. It's a hard question. Take some time to think about it." The therapist communicates that a response of "I don't know" is absolutely legitimate. This involves both attitude (believing that "not knowing" is a legitimate, serious response to difficult questions) and procedure (ability to wait during a silence for the client's next response).

Here is an example of recognizing and joining with the client from a demonstration tape (Miller, 1999). After talking earlier in the session about how he loved to go fishing, the client said, "I've got a big fish tank, 135 gallons." The therapist replied, "Oh, wow, fresh or salt water?" This brief response enhanced the therapeutic alliance in several ways. It communicated a shared knowledge about fish tanks (that they can have fresh or salt water), admiration (for its size), and attention to detail that was important to the client. In a conversation about the process after the session, the therapist, Scott Miller, expressed his belief that the time spent talking with the client before the "formal work" began was extremely important: "That was probably the most useful part of the therapy. We talked about fishing. We talked about what he did for a living. We chit chatted." An observing therapist, Kjos, commented that the time spent talking about fishing related to the client's wanting to see the therapist again. Miller agreed that this was probably the case. It should be noted that although a solution-focused perspective is clearly one component of Miller's approach, Miller described his approach not as solution-focused but as "client-directed, outcome-informed."

Highlighting strengths as they emerge contributes to a strong therapeutic alliance and builds hope. The following example from de Shazer and Dolan (2007) illustrates this process:

Wife: Yes, I think we communicated better this week.
Therapist: How did you communicate better this week?
Wife: Well, I think it was Rich. He seemed to try to listen to me more this week.

Therapist: That's great. Can you give me an example of when he listened to you more?

Wife: Well, yesterday for example. He usually calls me once a day at work, and …

Therapist: Sorry to interrupt, but did you say he calls you once a day? At work?

Wife: Yes.

Therapist: I'm just a little surprised, because not all husbands call their wives every day.

Wife: He has always done that.

Therapist: Is that something you like? That you wouldn't want him to change?

Wife: Yes, for sure.

Therapist: Sorry, go on, you were telling me about yesterday when he called. (p. 8)[3]

This is an example of respectfully confirming that a behavior was desired and then highlighting it. Done in a couples session, almost as a parenthetical remark, *before* discussion of the problem, this comment communicated the following to both partners: "This is something special about you, something that not all couples do. This is something I already know about you and find really interesting."

There is research that suggests that focusing on client strengths contributes to the therapeutic alliance. Duncan (2010) summarized some research conducted by Gassman and Grawe (2006) on minute-by-minute analysis of sessions. The data revealed that more successful therapists focused on client strengths throughout the session, not just at the end. Duncan added that alliance ratings are among the best predictors of outcome. Why? It appears that a positive alliance increases client participation and resource activation.

In a discussion of some research on solution-focused therapy, Beyebach (2007), of the Salamanca, Spain, research group, pointed out that the data obtained from client assessment of the therapeutic relationship could not be meaningfully correlated with outcome because of too little variance in the data: All of the ratings were consistently at the high end of the scale. Half in jest, Beyebach remarked, "Spanish therapists are just so nice." However, it may not be just that Spanish therapists are "so nice" (although they are!). Rather, it may be that a collaborative, solution-focused approach maximizes the likelihood that the therapeutic alliance will be strong. As Wampold (2007) has noted, when that bond is stronger, the client will be more likely to work collaboratively to achieve the goal.

THE THERAPEUTIC ALLIANCE IN STRATEGIC SOLUTION FOCUSED THERAPY

As in other ways, the combined approach blends much of what has been discussed above. There is genuine interest in the person and the details of daily life, apart from the problem. The attitude conveyed is an expectation that clients have strengths, resources, and fascinating, interesting things about them, even if there is also significant distress, or if there are symptoms or a *Diagnostic and Statistical Manual of Mental Disorders* (*DSM*) (American Psychiatric Association, 2000) diagnosis. As J. Simon and Nelson (2007) pointed out, even people who have been described as having severe and chronic mental illness are "not their label"; they are unique and wonderful people. In strategic solution focused therapy, the therapist listens for resources and special things, because these will become building blocks for solutions that will grow from within. There is an attitude of curiosity, sometimes playful, with an expectation that something may emerge at the end of the session that neither therapist nor client might have predicted beforehand. In addition, that solution may be "outside the box," and it may not be obviously or directly related to the problem.

Interest in the client also extends to the description of the problem for the strategic solution focused therapist. The therapist accepts the client's description of the problem and the goal at face value and does not assume that the therapist "knows better." Belief in the client is the therapist's "default position": "I believe you. You've been through some tough times, and I want to see things as you do. I see you as a special person. Your struggles are definitely not the only—or from my perspective, most interesting—things about you."

Sessions of strategic solution focused therapy often begin with a set of questions described by George, Iveson, Ratner, and Shennan (2009). These questions ask the following: "What are your best hopes from coming here?" "What will let you know those hopes have been met?" "What parts of that are already happening?" The inquiry is both assessment and intervention, because it provides an opportunity to join with the client

39

and to build hope. The therapist may also ask about the "worst" thing a therapist could recommend. This inquiry provides important information about what the therapist might want to avoid or possible unsuccessful attempted solutions. This is immediately followed by asking about the opposite: what the best or most helpful message might be. "Best hopes" and "worst and best message" inquiry are described in more detail in other chapters.

The therapist also elicits information about things that have nothing to do with the problem, often with a request for "some interesting things about you." The therapist might say, "If I had the privilege of knowing you over time, over many years, instead of just a few minutes, what special thing might I discover about you?"

The following excerpt illustrates the beginning of a session with Cindy.[4]

Therapist: Hi, Cindy. Since you first called for this appointment, what's better or different?

Cindy: Not a lot. Well, the year's almost over. Only six more weeks till summer vacation!

Therapist: All right! So, what are your best hopes from coming here?

Cindy: Well, to tell you the truth, if it was just up to me, I might not be here. It was actually Dr. Young's idea for me to come here.

Therapist: Oh, I didn't know that. What was your reaction when she suggested it?

Cindy: Annoyed at first, I guess. I mean, it's getting harder and harder for me to function at work. I'm a teacher. It's the first time I ever let deadlines go by. I never did that before. I think it's more my health.

Therapist: So if coming here helps you, how will you know?

Cindy: I'm not sure.

Therapist: Hmm, how do you think Dr. Young would answer that question? What do you think her best hopes would be?

Cindy: Maybe that I would be able to differentiate physical from social causes. Maybe I wouldn't keep bothering her so much, wanting to go out on disability and all.

> *It is not clear if Cindy is a customer and, if so, for what. The therapist wants to get to know Cindy a little more. Maybe discovering some other things about her and what is important in her world will provide some clues about how to join with her and create a bond.*

40

Therapist: Can I switch gears for a few minutes? I want to ask you some things about you, interesting things that maybe don't have to do with what you're here about today.

Cindy: Well, I'm a teacher, for 25 years.

Therapist: Wow! What grade do you teach?

Cindy: Second grade. I love it. I mean, maybe not recently, but I really do love it.

Therapist: What's your favorite part?

Cindy: Oh, the interaction with the kids, definitely. My least favorite is the district expectations about testing. And the administration! I am *so* glad there are only six weeks left in this year. I am so overwhelmed. When school is out of the picture, finally, for a few months, my focus will be on family and home.

Therapist: What do you like to do when you're home, when work is out of the picture for a while?

Cindy: Well, when I'm normal, I love to garden. Just get out there in the dirt. But I'm not gardening now. We don't really have a house. We sold our home last fall, because of the financial thing. We're just renting a house now. It's hard, because home is important to me.

Therapist: Of course. What else do you like to do when you're not teaching or gardening?

Cindy: I like swimming. I still go to the gym from time to time. Swimming is the one thing that doesn't hurt. And reading.

Therapist: What do you like to read?

Cindy: Oh, fiction, mysteries.

Therapist: How fun! Cindy, if I had the privilege of knowing you over time, for many years instead of for, like, ten minutes, what's a special thing I might discover about you?

Cindy: I don't know.

Therapist: It's okay to guess. Or you might think about how someone who knows you and loves you would answer that question.

Cindy: I'm an easy person to share life with, to talk to. I'm not a judgmental friend.

Therapist: That's really special. Tell me about the important people you share your life with these days.

Cindy: Well, I live with my husband. He's Jay. He's a realtor. And with my son, Andy. He's 10. Jay is trying to revamp his work, but in this market, it's hard.

Therapist: That's for sure. What would you say are the greatest strengths in your marriage?

Cindy: We appreciate each other, and respect each other.

Therapist: And the challenges—since every marriage has both?

Cindy: Definitely our financial ruin because of Jay. He's a gambler, not in the sense of going to Las Vegas or anything, but in sense of being an entrepreneur, doing house flips. We're debating filing for bankruptcy.

Therapist: Who else are the important people in your life?

Cindy: Well I have two grown daughters. Lisa, she's married, she's here in town, and two grandchildren. They're five and three [Smiles]. Angela, the three-year-old, she helps when I start thinking life's not worth living. And Suzi has a live-in boyfriend. She's finally getting through college. She's fought depression, just like I have, but she's stable now. And I have some really neat friends. My parents are deceased, and my brother is deceased.

    I was married 16 years to the girls' dad, before I divorced him. And what's scary is that sometimes these days I think where I was in my first marriage parallels where I am now. See, my ex-husband dropped out of life, just decided not to work. It was my decision to leave, and I guess it was a good decision, but it brought problems, too. Sometimes I think about leaving Jay because I don't think this economic situation will teach him a lesson, and I worry about Andy's future. But divorce isn't that simple. It brings as many problems as it solves. And I do care about him. I really do. And I've got all my medical stuff.

Therapist: How do you cope with that?

Cindy: Well, it's not easy. I was just in my mid-20s when I first got diagnosed with arthritis. It's hit the joints. The pain, it comes and goes.

Therapist: What's different when it goes, when it's less bad?

Cindy: I'm not really sure. I really don't know what triggers worse times. I don't think it's just stress. And there's also fatigue, so much fatigue. It makes it hard to work full time. I used up all my sick leave. Now when I'm out, I'm out without pay. I asked Dr. Young if she could put me on disability, but she said no, that it's turned into fibromyalgia now, and she doesn't put people on disability for that. She thinks being out of work and at home all the time just makes it worse. And she thinks I'm depressed.

42

Cindy describes how she has struggled with depression since her teen-age years. She has taken Prozac on and off for many years, now pre-scribed by Dr. Young. She hates the fact that she is gaining weight and wonders if the Prozac is contributing to it. She may talk with a psy-chiatrist about that. Cindy continues that she came for "talk therapy" only once before, around the time of her divorce.

Cindy: I was a little unhappy with the therapist at the time.

Therapist: How come?

Cindy: Well, I went in really not wanting to get divorced. I wanted coping mechanisms. I wanted education to cope without divorce. And she didn't give me coping mechanisms. I think she helped me to see how bad it really was, and that divorce was necessary.

This is a clue about what might not be helpful from a therapist. The therapist decides that it's time to ask the "worst and best message" question.

Therapist: Can I ask you a strange question?

Cindy: Sure.

Therapist: What's the worst thing I could say to you today? And I don't mean necessarily me, but that some therapist could say, that would make you go, "See, I knew it doesn't help to go talk to anyone"?

Cindy: This is a really stupid answer, but what I thought of was: You just need to do what's best for you.

Therapist: What makes that a stupid answer?

Cindy: I don't know. Maybe that everyone says you have to do what's best for you. And of course I do. But I don't want to look at my life from just my perspective. I want to see the big picture. It's not just about me. Maybe I have to adjust my expectations. Maybe mine are skewed.

Therapist: And what would be the opposite of that, the best or most help-ful, that would make you feel like you got what you need and want?

Cindy: Maybe help me look at big picture from outside. I feel like I've got blinders on, like I'm seeing through blinders, like all I see is— I've lost my home, I'm financially ruined, and I don't feel well.

43

> *Blinders: This is Cindy's image, her language. Maybe using it will lead to something that might make a difference. How the therapist builds on this language to continue the conversation is described in Chapter 7.*

At the conclusion of the initial session, the strategic solution focused therapist provides feedback that includes a validation component. As described in Chapter 2, this input includes *validation, compliment,* and *suggestion* components. How this feedback is planned is covered in more detail in later chapters, but it should be noted here that it is designed to strengthen the therapist–client bond. The validation communicates empathy and caring. It conveys that the therapist has heard the client and is attempting to understand. A nonjudgmental attitude of concern is communicated. The compliment summarizes strengths and may refer to "pieces of the solution" that are already happening. As noted earlier in this chapter, clients appear to benefit most when strengths are highlighted throughout a session and not just at the end, so this is certainly not the first time in the session that strengths have been mentioned. The compliment may highlight strengths previously described and add some additional perspectives. (It should be noted that the therapist does not typically use the word compliment; that is just the model's descriptive term for that component.) Finally, the suggestion invites amplifying what works, doing something different—or both. There is an attitude of respectful curiosity, perhaps playfulness, with an expectation for change that contributes to hope, that powerful change-promoting variable.

STAGES OF COMPETENCY IN CREATING THERAPEUTIC ALLIANCES IN THE SOLUTION-FOCUSED AND STRATEGIC THERAPIES

As with every competency, therapists vary in their ability to create alliances that promote change. The beginner may not assess readiness for change or client factors, erroneously assuming that every client is a customer—or that clients who are *not* customers cannot benefit from treatment. Beginners and advanced beginners may not spend sufficient time joining with clients, or they may make the joining into too much of a social conversation. For therapists who are new to the solution-focused and strategic therapies but knowledgeable about traditional psychiatry and other psychotherapy models, it may be difficult to focus on variables beyond traditional *DSM* diagnosis.

At the level of basic competency, solution-focused and strategic therapists usually attend to the relationship and readiness for change. They recognize that "one size does not fit all" and that "nothing works for everyone" (Norcross, 2005). However, they may miss the more subtle nuances or shifts in the relationship or client stance. At the higher levels of competency, therapists join with clients in creative ways. The timing of an empathic statement may be more precisely placed, and therapists may hear and use language and metaphors in more sophisticated ways. They may notice shifts in the relationship more quickly, a topic described in more detail in the next chapter.

Creating the therapeutic alliance comes more easily to some therapists than to others. The author remembers an intern who, although still approaching minimal competence in other domains, already demonstrated a high level of proficiency in establishing therapeutic relationships. This intern described how, before going to the waiting room to receive her client, she thought about welcoming this person as the most important person in the world right now. There was an advanced degree of attunement with the affect of the person, often reflected in a broad smile.

More highly proficient solution-focused and strategic therapists use language in a special way. They listen to it carefully and then match it. Dolan described how one master therapist, de Shazer, demonstrated respect and invited hope by using language carefully and intentionally. In addition, he made the process *look* easy (Dolan, as cited in de Shazer & Dolan, 2007).

A description of another master therapist, Berg, captures the combination of knowledge, method, and attitude emphasized throughout this book:

> [D]espite her relaxed demeanor and soft, restful tone of voice, she is completely focused on the client every second, fully absorbed and aware of every nuance, every word, careful not to miss any hint about what he or she is wanting from the session, attentive to every explicit or implicit reference to struggles, longings, dreams, goals, resources, strengths, and fragile hopes.
>
> And yet she makes it look easy. This perhaps should not surprise us, as the paradoxical combination of apparent ease and fully absorbed attention is also characteristic of master performers in other fields. Watching the musician Yo-Yo Ma, who is very technically skilled, one often has the

impression that he is simply enjoying himself playing the cello, and then it occurs to you that what you are hearing is technically and artistically perfect. He makes it look so easy. (de Shazer & Dolan, 2007, p. 38)

In summary, the solution-focused and strategic therapies create and enhance the common factors. In multiple ways, therapists build the therapeutic alliance. They join with the client and listen for best hopes (and worst fears). They identify important position variables, strengths, and resources, and they often highlight pieces of the solution that are already happening, thereby creating hope and promoting change.

NOTES

1. Fisch and Schlanger (1999) noted that all names and identities in the clinical examples in their book are fictitious.
2. From *Brief Therapy With Intimidating Cases*, by R. Fisch and K. Schlanger, 1999, San Francisco, CA: John Wiley & Sons, Inc., pp. 34–35. Copyright by John Wiley & Sons, Inc., 1999. Reprinted with permission of John Wiley & Sons, Inc.
3. From *More Than Miracles: The State of the Art of Solution-Focused Brief Therapy*, by S. de Shazer and Y. Dolan (with H. Korman, T. Trepper, E. McCollum, and I. Berg), 2007, New York, NY: Hayworth, p. 8. Copyright by Hayworth/Taylor & Francis Books. Reprinted with permission of the publisher.
4. Client names and identifying detail in the author's clinical examples throughout this book have been changed to safeguard client confidentiality.

4

Maintaining an Effective Therapeutic Alliance

This chapter covers how solution-focused and strategic therapists attempt to nurture therapeutic relationships that work for clients throughout treatment. It addresses three of the competencies in the domain of relationship maintenance: (a) addressing resistance and ambivalence, (b) recognizing and repairing therapeutic alliance ruptures, and (c) addressing the phenomena of transference and countertransference. The chapter describes how to regularly check in with clients about how things are going in the work together, using both formal rating scales and ongoing discussion. Therapists are encouraged to ask questions such as "Are we where we should be?" and "What might we be doing differently?" Talking about these things openly, with fluctuating feelings, discomfort, and ambivalence viewed as normal rather than "deal breakers," is "doing what works" in the therapeutic relationship—and it provides practice for the client's relationships outside therapy as well. Case examples illustrate ways of addressing ruptures in the therapeutic alliance both by "going back to the basics" and by "doing something different."

TREATMENT-INTERFERING FACTORS

The last chapter talked about treatment-*promoting* factors. If some things facilitate change, it makes sense that other factors can interfere with it.

Because building on what works and changing what does not form the cornerstones of a "doing what works perspective," preventing, recognizing, and resolving obstacles are also components of solution-focused and strategic practice.

Why don't psychotherapy clients change? Linehan (1993) talked about treatment-interfering factors that refer to things the client does (or does not do), such as missing appointments, arguing with the therapist, or not talking at all. However, client behavior is not the only thing that can interfere with therapy. Sperry (2010b) suggested that there are four kinds of treatment-interfering factors. One type comes primarily from the *client* (ambivalence, behaviors, attitudes). A second type comes mostly from the *therapist*; errors or negligence are examples here. A third source is the *client–therapist relationship*, when there is a breakdown of the collaborative alliance (and the need for both parties to participate in the repair). Sperry included transference and countertransference factors in this category. Finally, the difficulty may arise from the *intervention* or the treatment. Difficulties in scheduling and interference from factors outside the therapy, such as medical conditions and issues in the social system, fall into this category.

PREVENTING RUPTURES

The best way to resolve ruptures is to prevent them from happening in the first place! Of course, this is not always possible. However, maintaining both the *attitudes* and *behaviors* discussed in Chapter 3—joining with clients, listening, believing them, seeing them as resourceful, competent people, finding out and honoring what they want—can prevent many ruptures. When obstacles do arise, going back to those basics can help to get the relationship and the treatment back on track much sooner.

This book has already introduced the strategic solution focused tool that inquires about the worst—and then the best—things a therapist might say. The client's response to this "best and worst message inquiry" immediately alerts the therapist to things that may facilitate or interfere with treatment. What clients say about any previous episodes of treatment provides similar information. For instance, Julie complained that her employee assistance provider (EAP) "just listened." She said, "That was a total waste of time. I can get that from my girlfriends. I need some direction, some fresh ideas." Brad had a different perspective. "The worst thing you could do? Advice, some 'helpful Henry' coming in with some brilliant idea." What would help Brad to feel that he had gotten just what he needed? "Listening. I need a place to vent, rant and rage, if I need to." As Norcross (2005) has said, nothing works for everyone.

A strategic solution focused therapist at the earlier stages of competency might struggle with a response like Brad's. He or she might wonder how one can introduce a miracle question or inquire about attempted solutions with a client who has so specifically said that he wants to "vent." "Doesn't that mean I'm doing client-centered therapy, not strategic solution focused therapy?" a trainee might ask. At the higher levels of competency, the therapist might recognize that Brad has already described an unsuccessful attempted solution: "advice" or unwanted input. The therapist will be sure to provide plenty of time for Brad to express his feelings. There might be a comment that reflects the fact that Brad knows what helps him. In addition, the therapist might ask, "And when our conversation gives you that space, to vent, to be heard, in just the way that helps you, what will you start to notice?" Variations of solution-focused inquiry are discussed in more detail in subsequent chapters.

Doing what works to take care of the therapeutic relationship requires constant listening. Bliss (2010) called it "extreme listening" and said that this involves "going into a session with no idea about what needs to be discussed or what the outcome of the session ought to be" (p. 111). As Dolan (2009) has pointed out, the therapist does not really know what question has been asked (or heard) until the client has answered it. Listening to each response guides the therapist about where to go next—and it provides an opportunity for clarification and repair.

MONITORING THE RELATIONSHIP

"How are we doing?" "Are you and I where we should be?" "What else should we be doing or talking about?" These are questions that the therapist wants to ask, both at the first session and throughout a course of therapy. Some clients will not spontaneously tell us when we are off the mark; they just do not return. But when asked, sometimes they will give us feedback. This enables the therapist, in the spirit of the doing what works philosophy, to do something different.

In addition to ongoing discussion about how therapy is going, the therapist can use of one of the formal rating scales that are currently available. Duncan (2010) described the importance of obtaining client feedback about "fit" (alliance, approach) as well as "benefit" (Is the treatment working?). This critical information enables the therapist to be attuned to client preferences. It encourages flexibility and invites discovery of what works. Duncan wrote: "Client feedback is the compass that provides direction out of the wilderness of negative outcomes and average therapy ... significantly accelerating your development as a therapist and helping you become a better one" (p. 15). He added, "Continuous client feedback permits a practical process in which clients proactively shape our behavior until we get it right with them" (p. 17).

In his discussion of monitoring the therapeutic alliance, Duncan (2010) pointed out that lower ratings, especially early on, are actually a positive thing. The therapist wants the client to feel comfortable enough to tell the therapist where he or she can do something different. This is not like the car dealership example discussed in Chapter 1, where the request is for "a perfect score." This is the important *attitudinal* component again: The therapist *wants* to know what is not working.

There are some clients who will talk more openly about how things are going in a discussion with the therapist, whereas others will be more honest on a computer-based or pencil-and-paper rating. As with so many other things, one size does not fit all. Specific tools for monitoring both outcome and the therapeutic alliance are described in Chapter 8. But whatever the method used, seeking *feedback* is consistent with the "local clinical scientist" model (Stricker & Trierweiler, 1995) used in many practice settings. Early detection and discussion of potential problems is a desirable thing in the solution-focused and strategic therapies.

RESISTANCE: STRATEGIC AND SOLUTION-FOCUSED PERSPECTIVES

Clients sometimes do not participate in therapy the way their therapists hope they will. They may miss appointments, they may not express feelings, and they may not complete homework. Many models describe these behaviors as *resistance*. Solution-focused and strategic therapists see it differently. de Shazer (1984) wrote about "the death of resistance." What many other models call resistance is seen by solution-focused and strategic therapists as the client's unique way of cooperating. The attitudes of acceptance and not pathologizing emerge in this perspective. There is an assumption of a cooperative stance rather than an adversarial one.

de Shazer and Dolan (2007) said that what has been described as resistance often reflects people's natural protective mechanisms and realistic caution about changing too quickly. It may also result from therapist error, when an intervention does not match the client's situation or readiness for change. In addition, actually completing any homework given is not always important in these models. Homework may sometimes be given as a metaphor. It may be optional, or it might invite curiosity, noticing, or "changing slowly." Some strategic homework invites deliberately intensifying the symptom. Whether the client does the task or not, it is the client's *response* to it is that is useful. That response always provides valuable information about what is relevant and about what the client is prepared to do.

The client's degree of reactance may also be relevant here. According to Brehm's (1966) theory of psychological reactance, it is sometimes very important to people to maintain their freedom of choice. People differ regarding how much they tend to follow instructions, as opposed to "marching to one's own drummer." This may be one quality that the therapist wants to assess. People who are low in reactance may follow direct suggestions; those who are high in reactance may be better candidates for some strategic suggestions, including "restraint from change" input and feedback that maintains client autonomy. Therapist error in failing to assess or match the degree of reactance may account for why homework was not done.

AMBIVALENCE

Ambivalence is definitely not a problem for solution-focused and strategic therapists. Just the opposite is the case: Ambivalence is considered a valuable, universal construct and often a critical "ingredient of the solution." People are often distressed by their mixed feelings. They may consider them to be "the problem." As Quick (2008) pointed out, "Don't be so wishy-washy. You must decide!" often becomes an unsuccessful attempted solution, and an important alternative often includes permission for confusion.

Strategic solution focused therapy may include a "lesson" on "Ambivalence 101" (Quick, 2008) that specifically teaches about mixed feelings and how normal they are. The therapist may model how one can appropriately verbalize ambivalence, both about everyday dilemmas ("I want to sleep in and I don't want to get in trouble for being late") and about here-and-now reactions ("Part of me wants to suggest a new thought, and part of me isn't sure if that's something you're wanting right now"). Taking all the time one needs to make a decision and expecting mixed feelings (both about issues in one's life and about coming to therapy) may be suggested at the end of the session. Mixed feelings are valuable to consider in discussions of the therapeutic relationship, length of therapy, and relapse prevention and management. Rather than being seen as something to be eliminated, ambivalence may be actively recommended, and it may become part of the shared language of solution-focused and strategic therapy.

TRANSFERENCE AND COUNTERTRANSFERENCE: SOLUTION-FOCUSED AND STRATEGIC PERSPECTIVES

Transference and countertransference are not often discussed in the solution-focused and strategic therapies. Korman directly stated that "what happens in therapy should never be an important subject in the therapy sessions. It's what happens between the sessions that … is important to talk about" (2010, p. 212). However, other solution-focused and strategic therapists have observed that even if these constructs are not central in the model, distortions in perceptions and strong reactions to therapists—and clients—do occur and need to be addressed. In a discussion of client verbalizations to which solution-focused therapists need to be prepared to respond, Gorden (2010b) included "You obviously don't care about me" and "I am really attracted to you right now." Gorden suggested an exercise for supervision groups where participants brainstorm both the "worst things one could hear during a session" and possible responses. He noted that therapists commonly feel relieved to learn that other therapists worry about similar things. Just as solution-focused therapists ask future-oriented questions of their clients, solution-focused supervisors can invite trainees to create solutions from their strengths, in combination with the details of the individual situation.

For the "You don't care" situation, Gorden (2010b) suggested these possible responses: "How would [an] observation team know that I cared about you?" "How would your life be different if you knew I cared?" Here is a possibility for the "attraction" situation:

> I'm flattered by your reaction … of course, our lives aren't arranged for a relationship outside of here to be an option … but your reaction tells us that the part of you that can feel that attraction isn't broken. I'm looking forward to that part showing itself in your life outside of here very soon.

Transference has traditionally referred to the client's transfer of feelings and reactions from other situations and relationships (both past and present) to the therapy and the therapist. In countertransference, therapists transfer feelings and reactions to the client. Both transference and countertransference can be positive or negative. Keisler (2001) differentiated between subjective and objective reactions. In the objective reactions, the client (or therapist) may be reacting to very real characteristics of the other person, not just reenacting past or outside experiences. Sometimes this kind of countertransference is called a *counterreaction*.

Of course, in many situations, there are both subjective factors (those that truly are an enactment of other experiences) and real components. A client may feel like "people don't really care about me," and the therapist may, in fact, be excessively focused on completing agency paperwork right now. Or a therapist may feel bored during a session, with the fleeting thought of "I hope he doesn't want to reschedule." The therapist may want to consider, "Is this me? Am I reacting because this person reminds me of someone else in my past or present life, or is it because I'm overwhelmed at work? Or is this person objectively boring? Do I lack the skills needed right now to respond appropriately and empathically from a solution-focused or strategic perspective?"

Sperry (2010a) pointed out that different approaches may tend to elicit different client reactions. This may occur because there is a "grain of truth" in the client's complaint, with clients reacting to the styles and tools of the model used. A strategic therapist's client might complain that "my therapist suggests weird things," and a solution-focused therapist's client might have a negative reaction to "my therapist always being so damn positive." These reactions might be particularly strong when the client has a preexisting sensitivity and/or the therapist fails to tailor treatment to unique client characteristics and preferences.

TRANSFERENCE: EXAMPLES

Clearly, different people respond to the same therapist in different ways. The author routinely asks clients how they wish to be addressed, adding that "You can call me either Ellen or Dr. Quick, whichever you prefer." In addition to those choices, the following have also been chosen: Doctor, Dr. Ellen, Miss Ellen, Doc, Shrink, EQ, Ms. Quick, Dr. Fast, and Dr. Quack. One could speculate about the transference implications of that last one!

Lisa came to therapy for "OCD hoarding." She collected recipes, magazines, shoes, and activities, with little room in her apartment or her life for all of them. She attended multiple support groups and contacted multiple therapists, hoping that one of them would provide an answer. Everyone told Lisa to "get rid of things," and she told herself that, too. That remained an unsuccessful attempted solution. Lisa's therapist commented to her that she seemed to be collecting therapists in the same way that she collected other things in her life. Lisa had not looked at it that way before. The therapist and Lisa discussed how Lisa could "do something different" in how she utilized her therapists and how this might be a metaphor for collecting differently in other areas as well.

Here is an example of a session where the client heard therapist input through her own fears and concerns. Nancy was building up her courage to fly. She currently worked as a server at an upscale restaurant, and she dreamed of owning her own restaurant someday. Now she had an opportunity to attend a by-invitation-only cooking course in southern France. She had scraped together the money for the airfare and tuition, and she was determined to get there. Nancy had learned from the Internet about deliberately bringing on the feelings of panic. "That's so different from anything I tried before," she said. Together Nancy and the therapist did jumping jacks during the session, creating breathlessness.

But today Nancy was discouraged. "Now I have a new fear: that I'll get there fine but then panic and not be able to get back home." She imagined a bad flight from southern France to Paris, followed by tears at the airport and a huge panic attack while boarding the flight to New York. "How will you get through that?" the therapist asked. Nancy did not know. The therapist wondered aloud whether Nancy might want to research hotels near Charles de Gaulle Airport, in case there was any reason to postpone her flight for a day. (This may have been an error. Given more time, Nancy might have created her own solution.)

Nancy stared at the therapist. "You think I won't be able to fly out of Paris, don't you?" she said slowly. That had *not* actually been the therapist's thought, and the therapist told Nancy that. Nancy's face softened. "You're right," she said. "That comes from me, and from my critical husband, not from you." However, now that they were discussing it, the therapist commented that there were actually multiple reasons one might want or need to stay overnight near the airport, including delays on the connecting flight, over-booking, weather, terror threats, illness, and simply wanting to wait a day, as well as panic. The therapist added that one cannot have too many safety nets in place. Nancy agreed that this was true, adding that the names and phone numbers of some airport hotels might help her feel more in control.

The next week, a volcano in Iceland erupted. The media featured story after story about flight cancellations and mad rushes for airport hotel rooms. Nancy laughed. "If my trip were this week, I'd be the first one with a room," she said. (The volcano settled down by the time of Nancy's trip, two months later. She did not use her list of Charles de Gaulle Airport accommodations.)

COUNTERTRANSFERENCE

Because solution-focused and strategic therapists ask about the details of the client's situation, there is the possibility of becoming "too interested" in those details that are most interesting to the therapist, because of either longstanding issues or current personal interests. Larry was a drywall installer. His therapist happened to be in the process of remodeling his home and was just beginning to learn about drywall. This therapist took pride in always taking some time to chat with clients about their lives and interests. He liked Larry and found it easy to join with him, but he also noticed himself asking a bit more than usual about Larry's work. The therapist recognized this, and during solution elaboration, he was extra careful to make sure he was following Larry rather than using the session for his own curiosity and gratification.

In strategic therapy, reactions to a client are typically addressed from a one-down position, in combination with sharing one's genuine reaction. R. Fisch (personal communication, 1993) described working with a man who was pacing the room and shouting loudly. The therapist quietly said that he was feeling anxious right now and that when he got anxious, he did not think very clearly and that, as a result, he probably would not be of much help to his client.

The next example illustrates another therapist reaction that might be considered primarily an objective counterreaction. Melody had alienated most of the people in her life and, unfortunately, her therapist did not like her very much, either. Melody lied to her boss, her sister, and her daughter. She used therapy mostly to complain about how unfair life was. The therapist noticed herself referring to Melody in case conferences as "the person no one likes," and she always winced a little when she saw Melody's name on her schedule. She had considered using her own reaction as a tool in the therapy but had not been sure about how to do so in a helpful manner. At the end of a session, Melody asked if a certain appointment the next week was available. It was not, because that slot was reserved for first-time clients. Later that day the therapist noticed that Melody was scheduled in that slot and asked the clinic receptionist how that had happened. The receptionist responded that Melody had told her that "my therapist said that usually it's for first-time people, but next week I can have it."

The therapist felt a flash of anger. That feeling was followed by the realization that now she was ready to talk to Melody directly about the feelings elicited by Melody's behavior. The therapist brought it up at the next session:

Therapist: I was surprised to see you in this slot today, Melody.

Melody: Yeah, your gal just offered it to me last time.

Therapist: Actually, she didn't.

Melody: Yes, she did.

Therapist: No, Melody, she didn't. I checked with her, and she told me that you had told her that I had said you could have it. I had a bunch of different reactions when I heard her say that. I was angry, because that *wasn't* what I had said. And I also realized that you really felt you needed this appointment. And there was another piece. I felt like—Wow, this is how Melody's sister must feel when she asks you not to shop on eBay from her computer and you do it, and then you say you didn't. And I realized I needed to talk to you about it, even if it would be uncomfortable for both of us. Our relationship is too important *not* to talk about it.

This interaction became a turning point in Melody's treatment. Melody and the therapist talked about how lying "works" on one level but not on another, when it erodes relationships. Melody still struggled with honesty, but at many subsequent sessions she answered the question of "What's better or different?" with an example of a time when she had told the truth.

56

RECOGNIZING AND ADDRESSING RUPTURES IN THE SOLUTION-FOCUSED AND STRATEGIC THERAPIES

Misunderstandings and rifts can occur in all relationships—and relationships between solution-focused and strategic therapists and their clients are no exception. How the therapist manages relationship difficulties provides an opportunity for the client to see—and participate in—doing what works. This can help the therapy in three important ways. First, it may prevent clients from terminating therapy before their goals have been met. Second, it provides an opportunity, in the spirit of the strategic solution focused philosophy, for the therapist to change whatever was not working—in intervention or style or in other ways. Third, it provides an opportunity for the client to "do what works" "in here." The client can then be invited, in the spirit of building on what works, to experiment with similar responses "out there," in life outside of therapy. Melody's situation illustrated this.

Sometimes the client and therapist can "repair" the situation during the session. For example, Hazel was angry because her therapist was late for the session. The therapist apologized. The delay had been the result of another client's emergency, but that did not change the fact that Hazel had been kept waiting. After expressing how today was now "a total waste," Hazel went on to use the session as she usually did. At the end of the session, the therapist again apologized for the inconvenience. He also commented how much he had appreciated Hazel's speaking up directly about it, adding that he was struck by her ability to express her feelings and then move on to other topics. This was an example of "not having to wait for everything to go perfectly in order to create positive change." "Not that I hope people keep you waiting a lot," the therapist said, "but when they do, I guess I want to give you a gentle nudge to handle it like you did in here today, to express it and then not let it become a deal breaker or stop you from doing the stuff you were going to do." If Hazel could reenact her good management of frustration and discomfort in future situations and relationships, that would be a wonderful kind of "transference."

Christine began her second session by announcing, "I don't like that 'If it feels good, do it' thing you told me about last time. I mean, I don't think it's okay to go do drugs or cheat on my boyfriend or just stay home from work if I feel like it." Christine's therapist had *intended* to introduce the "doing what works perspective." What Christine *heard* was very different. Fortunately, she said so directly and early enough for the therapist to clarify—and to "own" the error of not checking out what was heard when the idea was initially introduced. Discussing how things that "feel good" sometimes don't work in spite of the immediate pleasure became a theme of this course of treatment.

"How can I best help?" This is not just a question to be asked at the beginning of treatment; rather, it is addressed in an ongoing way. It never substitutes for extreme listening, but it supplements and augments it. The therapist may be unsure whether the client wants to focus on something or has mentioned it in passing. Or it might be unclear whether a gentle nudge toward action or a message to "take your time" (or both, or neither) would be most helpful right now. The therapist does not have to guess. He or she might even acknowledge that "here comes that question again": What would be of the most help right now? And when the answer is "I don't know," the therapist can acknowledge that this is absolutely a legitimate response. Sometimes people truly *do not* yet know what will help most—and that is true for both clients and therapists.

Solution-focused and strategic solution focused therapists need to recognize that solution-focused can become "solution forced" for some clients. Nylund and Corsiglia (1994) and Lipchik (1994) have described this phenomenon. Especially at the beginning levels of competency, therapists who are learning to be solution-focused sometimes become so intent on discovering solutions that they forget to listen. Sometimes people want to "tell their story" and to express pain, anger, or other feelings before they are ready to consider solutions. At higher levels of competency, therapists recognize when to move slowly. They know that focusing on solutions does not mean becoming "problem phobic" and ignoring what the client needs right now.

Lipchik (1994) described a young woman who was devastated because her boyfriend had left her. She desperately wanted him to come back. Her therapist encouraged the client to imagine a time when she was feeling better. The only thing the client could imagine was the boyfriend's return, which was not likely to occur. When the therapist continued to press for a "different miracle," the client became increasingly upset and left abruptly. She never returned to the therapist.

How might a strategic solution focused therapist at a higher level of competency respond differently in this situation? There might be immediate recognition that he or she had become solution forced: that pushing for a solution that the client was not ready to envision has become an unsuccessful attempted solution. The therapist might acknowledge this openly.

"Leading from behind," the therapist might realize that this client may need time to cry and mourn. Telling her story, taking the time needed to heal, or taking good care of herself might all be goals for this client. Or the therapist might ask the client what will help her most right now. At the higher levels of competency, the therapist will believe that the client knows what she needs right now and listen for ways to facilitate that.

Here is another situation that might be handled differently by therapists at different stages of competency. An intern described difficulty ending sessions on time with a client who elaborated long and interesting responses to the therapist's miracle question inquiry. The client ignored comments such as "We have to wind down in a few minutes." She continued with future scenarios that were creative, and she seemed so engaged in the process that the intern was hesitant about interrupting her. The supervisor encouraged the intern to describe how he would end the session if he had an interview for his postdoctoral placement in an hour. The intern quickly realized that he did not have to wait for that interview in order to be clearer with his client about the need to stop for now, and his skills and confidence about managing his schedule grew quickly.

As noted in previous chapters, strategic solution focused therapy sessions typically end with feedback that includes validation, compliment, and suggestion/input components. When clients have expressed concerns about the therapeutic alliance, the therapist can openly acknowledge these concerns during this discussion. In addition, clients can be complimented on their willingness to talk about their concerns—and, when applicable, on their ability to cope with them and to incorporate them into the solution.

At his first session, Rod had talked about how hard it was for him to come to the clinic. The worst message someone could give him was that he was "a nut case" (as his ex-wife had repeatedly suggested). During his second session, a man's agitated sobbing was audible through the usually soundproof walls. The therapeutic alliance includes not just the client's relationship with the therapist but the full experience at the clinic.

For an instant Rod's face registered terror, quickly followed by a sneer of disgust. "Some loony losing it," he muttered. "That's hard to listen to," the therapist said softly. Both were silent for a few minutes. Then Rod spontaneously picked up where he had left off, and the conversation continued.

At the end of the session, Rod commented, "That poor bastard. I'm glad he settled down. I hope he's okay." The therapist again validated how hard the screams had been for both of them to hear. The therapist then told Rod, "I am struck by two things. You didn't let that sound stop you from continuing our conversation, and you clearly care about that other guy. Those two things feel huge to me."

Rod continued his therapy, and he grew gentler with himself as well.

As discussed in Chapter 3, agreement on the details and tasks of therapy is one component of the bond between therapist and client. Therefore, a rift can occur when scheduling and frequency of sessions become problematic. If not managed, scheduling problems can damage the therapeutic alliance, even if other things are going well.

Sam's answer to the "worst message" question was "You telling me that I'll have to wait a month to see you again." Unfortunately, that was exactly the situation for individual appointment availability at the clinic. "You have to go to a group" was also one of the worst things Sam could be told. The therapist told Sam that she was embarrassed about the wait for individual sessions. Groups were available, she said, but she knew that Sam did not think those would be helpful. Sam was put on a waiting list, but when appointments opened up, Sam was not available.

At his next session Sam told the therapist, "This every five week thing isn't working." The therapist empathized and checked her schedule again. It turned out that that a cancellation made another appointment available the next day. Did Sam want it? He did. "What's better or different?" the therapist asked at that next appointment. Several things were better. Sam had reached out to a friend and had started practicing his bass again. Sam wanted to stay on the waitlist. Before his next appointment, a few more cancellations opened up. They were offered, and Sam declined them, telling the receptionist, "Nah, it's just a little bit till my next appointment. That's okay." Sam and the therapist commiserated together about the availability of appointments. Sessions were not available as frequently as either of them would have liked, but the therapeutic alliance had been repaired.

Sometimes when clients are dissatisfied with therapy, it initially appears that the problem is with the therapeutic relationship. Careful inquiry about what will make a difference sometimes reveals that the *method* is what is not working. For example, Wendy complained that "this envisioning the future stuff we do" isn't helping me. "I can envision stuff, but I still don't know what I want." Together the therapist and Wendy reviewed what they had discussed in previous sessions. They both recognized that Wendy changed her area for change at every session—and the therapist had simply followed, asking a new miracle question every time. As Fisch, Weakland, and Segal (1982) have pointed out, treatment failures appear to occur more frequently when the area for change is unclear. The therapist and Wendy returned to problem clarification, and Wendy recognized that there were, in fact, multiple goals. Usually focus on one highest priority goal works better, but for Wendy, this was not a good fit. Permission to "not know what I want and to have more goals than I should" became the next step for Wendy. Monitoring how treatment is going and shifting gears are described in more detail in Chapter 8. But regardless of whether the difficulty is primarily a rupture in the relationship or a problem with the method, open discussion can transform a problem to an ingredient of the solution, becoming part of what works in the solution-focused and strategic therapies.

5

Performing an Integrative Solution-Focused and Strategic Assessment

This chapter discusses the two clinical competencies in the "intervention planning" domain related to assessment: how solution-focused and strategic therapists perform integrative assessments and how they view and use multiaxial *Diagnostic and Statistical Manual of Mental Disorders (DSM)* (American Psychiatric Association, 2000) diagnosis. There is discussion of problem clarification, with a focus on how something is a problem, who is the "customer," and "why now?" The chapter introduces solution elaboration and "best hopes inquiry" as assessment tools, and it covers scaling questions and assessment of the client's strengths and "theory of change." "Exceptions" or "times when the problem isn't" are investigated in this approach, and "attempted solutions" and whether they are "working" well enough are also assessed. The chapter considers how solution-focused and strategic assessments are both similar to and different from the kind of assessment done in some other models, with discussion of assessing safety and systemic issues.

Comprehensive assessment plays an important role in case conceptualization and treatment planning, which are discussed in the next chapter. Traditionally, assessment includes systematic evaluation of multiple domains. Sperry (2010a) provided the following list of areas to be evaluated:

current problem and its context, current functioning, mental status, social variables, cultural variables (including cultural identity, level of acculturation, and perceptions of illness), developmental history (including personal and family dynamics), medical history (including past mental health treatment), health behaviors, resources, and expectations for treatment.

Sperry (2010a) described three ways of obtaining information during an assessment. The therapist can be like an "investigator," discovering "what happened." Like a "travel planner," the therapist can explore the destination or goal, creating a map. Sometimes the therapist may also be like a "forecaster," and the forecast may include obstacles that could be encountered along the route. Sperry noted that therapists can use deductive reasoning, moving from the general to the specific, and/or inductive reasoning, moving from the specific to the general and synthesizing seemingly unrelated pieces of information. Sperry added that assessment can be symptom based, theory based, or pattern based. He noted that symptom-focused assessment may make things easy to measure but may miss the bigger picture, and theory-focused assessment may help therapists to integrate data but may become "therapist centered" and fail to capture the client's view. Sperry asserted that therapists at higher levels of competency tend to use multiple perspectives.

PROBLEM CLARIFICATION

In strategic therapy and strategic solution focused therapy, assessment typically begins with problem clarification. ("Pure" solution-focused therapists may focus less on the *problem*, moving more directly to focus on the *goal*.) Taking what Sperry (2010a) called the investigator stance, the strategic or strategic solution focused therapist attempts to clarify the complaint. If there are multiple issues, what is the highest priority? What happened that led up to this person's request for treatment? Like a journalist, the therapist asks "who, what, when, and where questions," often seeking dialogue and behavioral description of the complaint. There is also investigation of "Why now?" and "Who is the customer—and for what?" (Quick, 2008, p. 20). Description of details is encouraged and valued. Fisch and Schlanger (1999) pointed out that the strategic therapist might describe a problem in terms of behavior—such as "checking the stove 40 times a day"—rather than calling it "obsessive compulsive disorder" (in general).

It should be noted that problem clarification focuses on *complaints* rather than on symptoms. The fact that a behavior or symptom is "there" does not automatically make it a problem for a strategic or strategic solution focused therapist. Fisch and Schlanger (1999) noted that something becomes a problem only when someone complains about it. Quick (2008) encouraged inquiry about the *way* in which something is a problem. Is something problematic because there is "too much" or "too little" of some behavior? Or is the problem more one's thoughts or feelings about a state of affairs?

Samir complained that he changed jobs every 2 years. He worried that this might make him look "flaky" on his résumé, and he disliked the idea of "starting over" at accruing vacation and sick leave. A therapist at a lower level of competence might assume that there is sufficient information about how the job shifts are a problem. At higher levels of proficiency, the therapist will not assume that he or she knows.

"Samir," the therapist asked, "what's the main way that changing jobs so often is a problem for you?" "I just don't do stress well," Samir sighed. "It's so stressful, having to learn a new routine and deal with new people. I just hate it."

Like much of the inquiry conducted in the solution-focused and strategic therapies, problem clarification can become an intervention as well as being an assessment tool. Inquiring "In what way is this a problem?" frequently shifts how clients see the problem while simultaneously influencing what the therapist does. In Samir's case, this information led to practice seeking out and tolerating other kinds of stress. What matters is not the severity of a behavior from some external point of view but the client's perspective. This issue is addressed in more detail later in this chapter in the discussion of *DSM* diagnosis.

There are different degrees of competence in assessment of "Who is the customer—and for what?" For example, with a client who has initiated the request for an appointment, a therapist at the lower levels of proficiency might automatically assume that this person is self-referred and therefore a customer for change. At the higher levels of proficiency, the therapist may explore the "why now?" question in more detail. This inquiry may reveal that the call for an appointment followed a conversation with a partner, friend, doctor, or supervisor. That person may be the primary customer. The client may be a complainant or visitor—or a customer for something different from the concern of the "invisible referral source."

The following excerpt from a session with Carmen illustrates problem clarification. Carmen, age 28, has been married to Zach for 6 years.

They have a 5-year-old son, Ronnie. Carmen is an only child, and her parents, who moved to California from Guadalajara, Mexico, before Carmen was born, have been divorced for many years. Both parents live nearby, and Carmen has regular contact with both of them. Carmen describes multiple concerns: depression, sleeping either too much or not enough, weight gain, concern about her alcoholic mom being homeless, finances, arguing with Zach, and dealing with Ronnie (who is hyperactive and has a mild hearing loss and often "screams"). Carmen is a word processor in a county government office, and Zach drives a delivery truck for a local business. The company for which Zach works is not doing well and therefore often cuts his hours.

Therapist: Wow, Carmen, you sure do have a lot going on. So of all those things, which one is the most important to do something about?

Carmen: It's Mom, definitely Mom. She's alcoholic, and now she's homeless. She lost her apartment, and she calls me 25 times a day. That's truly not an exaggeration. She needs money. She needs a shower. She's burned every bridge she had. She hangs out outside my house, and I have to lock all the doors so she doesn't come in and take a shower. And she makes me feel so guilty. She tells me it's my fault she's sleeping in her car, that I'm a terrible daughter. I'm sick with guilt. I'm eating, and first I couldn't sleep at all, and then I went for a few weeks of just wanting to sleep all the time.

Therapist: Does that mean, then, that when something is different with Mom and how you're handling the situation, that's going to make a difference?

Carmen: Yeah, I think so.

As the session proceeds, the therapist learns that Carmen had called for an appointment after her mom had suggested that she might move in with them and babysit Ronnie. Because child care was so expensive, Zach had not immediately said "no" as vehemently as Carmen had hoped he would. Carmen began to feel that she was not only a bad daughter but also a selfish wife and mother. There are also hints about several attempted solutions: "Don't feel guilty" and "Be consistent in setting limits with Mom." Attempted solutions are more formally assessed later in this session.

SOLUTION ELABORATION

Solution-focused and strategic therapists regularly assess clients' goals, strengths, and best hopes for the therapy. In Sperry's (2010a) terms, they are taking a travel planner stance toward assessment. Like problem clarification, solution elaboration is both assessment and intervention. Miracle question inquiry, sometimes the original version and sometimes a variation, is routinely done by solution-focused and strategic solution focused therapists. (Pure strategic therapists may not regularly use this method, but they clearly do assess, in specific detail, what the client wants.) Miracle questions invite a picture of a desired future, elicit increasingly specific details about that scenario, and then inquire about parts of that solution that are already happening, or exceptions. As a therapist's level of proficiency grows, he or she becomes increasingly skilled at tailoring the timing and content of miracle question inquiry to clients' strengths, cultural variables, and preferences. de Shazer once said that he asked the miracle question when he was beginning to "see the miracle" in the details the client was describing (de Shazer & Dolan, 2007, p. 62). The process of using miracle questions for both assessment and intervention is illustrated further in later chapters.

Assessment in solution-focused therapy often includes scaling questions (Berg & de Shazer, 1993). Typically, this inquiry occurs after miracle question elaboration. As described in Quick (2008), here is an example of scaling question inquiry: "On a zero to ten scale, where zero is when you first called for an appointment, and 10 is that the miracle has happened, where are you right now?" For any response other than zero, the therapist asks, "How did you get to x?" "What else tells you you're at x?" The client's response provides useful information. Then the therapist asks what "$x + 1$" will look like. The client's answer again gives important, individualized ideas for client-generated homework or projects.

As a therapist's level of proficiency grows, scaling question inquiry becomes increasingly sophisticated. For example, a client who is at a 3 says that 4 will be "the miracle, just like I just said." The therapist would like to hear a smaller step and might say, "That sounds great! What would be the first little piece of it that you'll see?" Here are some other examples of higher-level scaling questions: "How confident do you feel that you can stay at that 3?" "What will tell you your confidence is now at a 4?" "What number would your husband give you?" "What do you know that he doesn't?" (This might be asked if the client's own number is higher than her guess about her husband's.) "What else?" "What else?" Solution-focused therapists routinely observe that the most useful responses often emerge after the fourth or fifth "What else?" Therapists at lower levels of proficiency may abandon their "What else?" questioning long before that!

BEST HOPES

The therapists at BRIEF, a British solution-focused training and practice center, have proposed a three-question model for eliciting clients' best hopes for therapy. This model can be used both by solution-focused and strategic therapists and by therapists of other orientations who wish to combine solution-focused and strategic tools with other methods. It is extremely useful for intake appointments.

Here are the questions, adapted from George et al. (2009):

1. What are your best hopes from coming here?
2. What will let you know that those hopes have been met (or that this was helpful)?
3. What are you already doing that might in some way contribute to those hopes being met? (or, What pieces of this are already happening?)

The BRIEF therapists note that the wording asks about "best hopes *from* our work" (or coming here). It is not best hopes *for*. This may sound like a fine point, but best hopes *for* can sound like an agenda for the session. Best hopes *from* is outcome.

It is not always easy for people to answer the best hopes question immediately or specifically. They give responses such as "I need to talk to someone" or "I'm depressed." The skilled therapist stays with the question. "So if talking to someone was helpful, what would that lead to?" Or, for "I'm depressed": "So, if coming here is helpful for the depression, in just the way you want, how will you know?" People often express their best hopes in general terms: "I'll be normal (or happier)." "We'll get along better." "I'll have more self-esteem." In response, the therapist asks: "What will you be doing then?" "Who will notice first?" "What else?" These questions funnel the initial general response into a more specific, behavioral picture, a picture that may include pieces that are actually already happening—and are first steps toward the goal.

Some clients' best hopes are for medicine. When this is the response, the therapist asks, "So if a doctor prescribes medicine for you, what will let you know that it's working?" "What else?" "What will your mother (wife, boyfriend) notice about you?" For other clients, their best hopes are for the therapist to be the gatekeeper, to get them into—or out of—something. The BRIEF therapists suggest that before addressing "Will we or won't we provide that gatekeeper function?" it is useful to clarify the preferred future or the goal. "So if your child got into that special class and was starting to learn, what would you see different?" "So if you didn't have to work with that supervisor, how would that make a difference?" If the client wants the therapist to be a gatekeeper for something that there actually is a procedure or set of criteria for evaluating, he or she can provide clear information about the process (for example, disability evaluation, attention deficit hyperactivity disorder [ADHD] protocol evaluation), and that becomes the next step in the plan.

Sometimes best hopes are unrealistic. "I want to not have to go to school." "I want my dad to stop drinking." "I want you to get my dental insurance to pay for orthodontia." BRIEF's therapists suggest the following perspective: Of course one would not want to encourage false hopes, but those hopes are in the client's heart anyway. The skilled therapist will ask a respectful, hypothetical question that takes the hopes seriously and simultaneously directs the focus toward the differences that achieving those hopes would bring. One can also ask clients what they think the chances are of that thing happening, because most clients do respond accurately. For example, a woman says, "I want my husband to come back," and the therapist asks, "What do you think the chances are of that happening?" not as a challenge, but with genuine, empathic curiosity. The client will probably give a fairly realistic answer. And if that answer is "none," that allows the therapist to legitimately ask: "What else would let you know that this process had been helpful?" The answer might involve mourning, going on, or getting support. There is a related—and wonderful—question that asks: "Do you have to wait for x to happen in order to make things better for you, or are there things you can do to make it better even while x is still going on?" (I. Berg, personal communication, July 17, 1992).

Some clients answer the best hopes question with "I don't know." The therapists from BRIEF say: Assume motivation—for something. Assume the following: When clients are there, even if under duress, they *do* have something they want—maybe to stop someone else from complaining, to stop their children from being taken away—something. If it was someone else's idea for the person to be here, the therapist might ask what the client thinks are the referring person's best hopes for the work. "So what would your wife hope would be different as a result of your coming here? What would she hope to see? And if she saw that, what difference would that make in your life?"

With children and families, the best hopes questions can be asked of every member of the system, assuming that even young children have answers. When responses from different family members (couples, children and parents) are the opposite of each other (such as one wanting more space and one wanting more time together), the therapist can acknowledge the differences. The family members are not so fragile that they will be destroyed by this being said openly. It is no secret to them that they disagree—that is probably why they are here. Sometimes the goal—and the treatment plan—include being able to talk about it openly, normalizing having differences, and being able to do the tasks of every day living and doing good things for themselves, and for each other, even in the presence of those differences.

"What are you going to remember, or take with you, from our conversation today?" This question assesses the "take-home message." It is extremely instructive, because what the client describes may be quite different from what the therapist thought was most important. The therapist may have thought that he made a creative, relevant suggestion, and the client may say "You listened." Or the session may have been a disappointment. Or some phrase or question that the therapist barely noticed may be the take-home message. What ever it is, it is important information, which will inform subsequent treatment planning (Quick, 2008).

As described in Chapter 3, another strategic solution focused assessment question asks: "If I had the privilege of knowing you really well, over time, over many years, what really special thing would I know about you, something that might not be immediately obvious? It's okay to guess." This question elicits information about strengths and unique characteristics from the client's perspective. Even people who are devastated, in crisis, agitated, or do not want to be there can usually answer that question. The information obtained here helps the therapist to individualize the treatment.

Asking about the worst and best things a therapist could say has already been described, and this is also part of strategic solution focused assessment. How can the therapist best help? The responses to these questions provide important information about multiple things: goals, the client's implicit (or explicit) theory of what will produce change, and nonhelpful messages given by others, including past therapists.

The next excerpt from the session with Carmen illustrates some of the inquiry described above.

Therapist: Carmen, what are your best hopes from coming here?

Carmen: To know how to deal with Mom, to deal with stress better.

Therapist: What will let you know that those hopes have been met?

Carmen: I'll feel relief, happier, more relaxed.

Therapist: And how will that show?

Carmen: Maybe I won't lose patience as much, and I won't worry so much about her.

Therapist: What's the worst message I could give you today? And I don't mean necessarily me, but that some therapist could say, that would make you go—"Yuck, that was a waste of time."

Carmen: Maybe not giving me any suggestions. If I go out of here and I still don't know what to tell her.

Therapist: And what would be the best, the most helpful?

Carmen: I want tangible words I can tell my mom, suggestions.

Therapist: Carmen, if I had the privilege of knowing you over time, over many years, what special thing might I discover about you?

Carmen: I don't know. I'm just an ordinary person.

Therapist: It's okay to guess. Or you might think about how someone who knows you and loves you might answer that question.

Carmen: [Pause] I think I have a good head on my shoulders. I like to understand things and think about them. And I'm determined. I can stick to things. Well, maybe not right now, with Mom and everything, but most of the time I can.

Therapist: Wow. What's an example of something you stuck to?

Carmen: Knowing that I would never drink. Seeing what it did to Mom and our family. And I've really stuck to that.

Therapist: That's huge. [Pause] Can I shift gears now, and ask you a strange question?

Carmen: Sure.

Therapist: I want to invite you to imagine that after we get done talking today, and you go home, and do whatever you're going to do the rest of today, and go to bed, and go to sleep tonight, that a miracle happens. And the miracle is that the problem you're

71

here about, being so stressed out about Mom, and not knowing what to say to her, is solved. It's tomorrow morning, Thursday, whatever time you get up. What's the first thing that's different, that lets you know this isn't a problem any more?

Carmen: Okay, the phone rings, it's Mom, she wants to come over, and I'll say "No. Not today."

Therapist: And Mom will respond … ?

Carmen: Oh, she'll just keep going.

Therapist: Of course!

Carmen: And I'll just say it again. "Not today." And Mom may hang up.

Therapist: Wow. What else will be different?

Carmen: Maybe I won't be upset. I'll tell Zach, "That was Mom, her morning call, and I said 'No.'" Zach will see that I mean it this time.

Therapist: What will let him know that?

Carmen: Maybe my tone. Not all wound up. Not crying. Not so guilty.

Therapist: And when you're not crying or all wound up or guilty, you're more … ?

Carmen: Quieter. Maybe talking nicer. Maybe not asking him to do so much. I'll just do it, just rinse out his glass. He'll see me as more level, less nagging.

Therapist: And when you do those things, how will Zach be different?

Carmen: Joke around more. He'll say "That's my babe," make that funny face he makes.

Therapist: And what will Ronnie notice about Mommy?

Carmen: How Mommy treats Daddy. Not arguing so much. When Daddy is watching cops, maybe Mommy is watching too!

Therapist: So suppose these good things continue, and then the doorbell rings, and it's Mom at the door. What will be different, as a result of all the good things that have been happening?

Carmen: Okay, Ronnie comes running up to me, "Lita's here, Lita's here. Can I play with Lita?" And I'll just stand there at the door, and I'll ask her to leave. "I asked you not to come today." And if she tries to push in, I'll just close the door, and ignore her crying. Ronnie will say, "Why is Lita crying?" and I'll tell him, "Ronnie, Lita's not feeling good today, and this isn't a good day for her to play with us."

Therapist: And what will you be thinking about when *is* a good day for Lita to play with us?

Carmen: Well, maybe Saturday, when Zach is working.

Therapist: How will you let Mom know that?

Carmen: Well, maybe I'll call her later, and say, "Hey Mom, let's get together at the park Saturday morning, you, me, and Ronnie." And if she calls between now and then, I'll say: "I'll see you Saturday."

As solution elaboration continued, Carmen was able to describe how she would respond to things Mom might bring up at the park, including pleas for money and an overnight visit. Carmen imagined saying, "No, this is about us spending time with Ronnie" and encouraging their "Lita games."

When the therapist asked if pieces of this scenario were already happening, Carmen said, "Actually, they are. I think I know what to say. That's what I needed." The therapist asked a scaling question, and Carmen was at a 6. "How did you get all the way up to a 6?" the therapist asked. Having a plan, Carmen responded. What would 7 look like? Actually doing it!

It might be noted that goals and progress toward goals are assessed in follow-up visits as well as initial ones. Strategic solution focused therapists often begin a session by asking, "What's better or different?" In ongoing problem clarification, they may also ask: "Where should we focus today? If our conversation helps you, in just the way you want, what should we be talking about today?" Sometimes clients bring up something totally different from the previous goal. The therapist certainly will not say, "Sorry, we can't talk about that. It's not on our list of goals." But he or she probably will want to check on whether the area for change has shifted and whether the goal from last time is still important. And if so, where is the client with it?

ATTEMPTED SOLUTIONS

Strategic and strategic solution focused therapists also assess attempted solutions. (As noted in Chapter 2, pure solution-focused therapists may not formally assess this variable, although in some situations, sophisticated solution-focused therapists clearly do consider this dimension.) This component of the assessment simply and directly asks, "What have you tried, in your best attempts to solve this problem?" The therapist may ask what other people have suggested and what the person has said to him or herself about the situation (there is some overlap with cognitive approaches here). Then there is inquiry about the effects of what has been tried. "What happened when you did that?" That is, what were the results? The therapist is listening to hear whether the attempted solution worked, important information for intervention planning.

At higher levels of proficiency, strategic and strategic solution focused therapists also listen for what Fisch et al. (1982) called the *basic thrust* of various attempted solutions. Fisch et al. gave the example of a client who has tried to solve an insomnia problem by first staying up late, then eliminating coffee, next getting sleeping pills, and then trying to go to bed earlier. These efforts might *seem* different from one another. "Going to bed earlier and staying up later are opposites," the beginning strategic therapist might say. At higher levels of competence, the therapist might recognize that all share the same basic thrust: "I am trying to make myself go to sleep." The data gathered here tells the therapist what to *avoid* during treatment planning. The attitude reflected during this part of the assessment involves looking beyond the specifics and being willing and even eager to "think outside the box." Therapists look at the kinds of patterns described by Sperry (2010a) earlier in this chapter.

The following excerpt from the session with Carmen illustrates the process of assessing attempted solutions.

Therapist: So what have you tried, before coming here, to deal with this tough situation with your mom?

Carmen: Well, I've talked to Dad. And he says, "It's not your problem. Don't feel guilty. You have people depending on you."

Therapist: And when he says that …

Carmen: It helps a little. I know he means well. But, I mean, he's got his own issues with her. I still feel so guilty. I can't just dump her like he did. But I'm also so ashamed of her. And then I get ashamed for feeling that way.

Therapist: Who else has suggested anything?

Carmen: Zach. He says if I don't want to let her in, just don't let her in. But sometimes I do, when he's at work. I just feel sorry for her, and she needs a shower. But then that just makes her ask for more, and then I yell at her, and I worry that Zach will find out I let her in, and then I feel even worse.

Therapist: Carmen, what have you said to yourself in your head about this?

Carmen: Oh, to be consistent, not to be such a wimp, and not to feel guilty. [She sighs and shakes her head.]

Therapist: Does that help you?
Carmen: No, I can't even do that right.

The information obtained here lets the therapist know that "Don't feel guilty" and "Be consistent in setting limits for Mom" are two attempted solutions. The messages come both from Carmen herself and from others. These attempted solutions are not working well enough. This information informs intervention planning, described in the next chapter.

OTHER VARIABLES ASSESSED

Because treatment is tailored to the individual, solution-focused and strategic assessment may also include investigating how clients feel about "homework"—whether it is called that or not. "How do you learn best?" the therapist may ask. "When you change something in your life, do you tend to do it gradually, or all at once, or both?" "Are you a writing person?" Some clients love to keep journals and love ideas for writing tools, and others hate writing. "Are you a person who usually tries out suggestions, or do you march to your own drummer in terms of knowing when a suggestion is right for you?" Questions like these assess the degree of reactance or wanting to maintain independent choice or "not being told what to do" (Brehm, 1966), as described in the previous chapter. The person who likes to keep his or her options open may respond better to "You can and don't have to ..." input and indirect or metaphorical suggestion than to direct suggestion.

There are questionnaires that systematically ask clients about strengths. Smock (2011) has developed the Solution Building Inventory, a more formal tool for solution-focused assessment. Instead of measuring pathology, it assesses variables such as awareness of exceptions, hope for the future, and confidence in one's problem-solving abilities. Some strategic solution focused therapists integrate principles and tools from positive psychology into their work (Bannink, 2010; Quick, 2008). One important positive psychology concept, *signature strengths*, refers to traits that people already possess and can use to enhance both meaning and coping. Peterson and Seligman (2004) categorized 24 character strengths and virtues. Signature strengths can be either formally or informally assessed.

As all therapists do, solution-focused and strategic therapists need to know whether there is a risk of danger to someone and, if so, they need to follow legal and ethical guidelines. This is addressed in Chapter 10 as well. Fiske (2008) described a solution-focused approach to preventing suicide, which includes assessment of "10 reasons for living," adapted from an instrument originally published by Linehan, Goodstein, Nielsen, and Chiles (1983). In settings where therapists are required to do formal suicide assessments, with detailed inquiry about risk factors, available weapons, symptoms, suicide plans, and past attempts, Fiske recommended spending at least as much time assessing reasons for living as reasons and means for dying. This could be considered a general principle in solution-focused and strategic assessment: to spend at least as much time assessing strengths as pathology—and preferably more.

HOW IS ASSESSMENT IN THE SOLUTION-FOCUSED AND STRATEGIC THERAPIES SIMILAR TO AND DIFFERENT FROM ASSESSMENT IN OTHER APPROACHES?

As discussed so far in this chapter, assessment in the solution-focused and strategic therapies gathers details about problems, goals, and attempted solutions. It includes best hopes inquiry and scaling questions. Strengths and special characteristics are assessed. Therapists assess position, the client's theory of change, and cultural variables (covered in more detail in Chapter 10). They may investigate the best and worst messages a therapist might give, and at the end of a session they may assess the take-home message.

One might ask: What about some of the other variables described by Sperry (2010a) and mentioned earlier in this chapter? These include developmental history (including personal and family dynamics), medical history (including past mental health treatment), health behaviors, and a formal mental status exam. In general, solution-focused and strategic assessment allows the client to determine how much detail feels important to share here. These areas may be less formally evaluated here than in other approaches to diagnostic assessment. There may be an expectation that the client will tell us what we need to know and how much detail in these areas is important to share. In a description of Steve de

Shazer, an expert solution-focused therapist, Dolan noted that although solution-focused therapy is best known for its future focus, de Shazer "combed through the client's full range of experiences in order to unearth, discover, or identify crucial exceptions … and significant resources that were necessary to solution-building" (de Shazer & Dolan, 2007, p. xi).

DSM DIAGNOSIS FROM A SOLUTION-FOCUSED AND STRATEGIC PERSPECTIVE

Solution-focused and strategic therapists do not typically think about clients in terms of their diagnoses on the five axes of the American Psychiatric Association's *DSM* (American Psychiatric Association, 2000). From one strategic perspective, a *DSM* diagnosis may actually distract the therapist (and the client) from what is most important: the behaviors "performed" in a specific interpersonal context and how others react to them. The fact that a particular behavior is present does not mean that it is always addressed in solution-focused and strategic therapy, even if other professionals have previously called it a "symptom" or diagnosed it. Duncan wrote: "Diagnosis in mental health is not correlated with outcome or length of stay … [It] cannot provide reliable guidance to clinicians or clients regarding the best approach to resolving a problem" (2010, p. 185). In their book subtitled *I Am More Than My Label*, solution-focused therapists J. Simon and Nelson (2007) described how clients who have received behavioral healthcare services for many years have far more complex and interesting characteristics (and victories in their lives) than their diagnostic labels might suggest.

However, just as solution-focused and strategic therapists attempt to understand their clients' contexts and "speak the client's language," they know that the larger system in which they work "speaks *DSM*." They therefore need to be knowledgeable about *DSM* criteria and able to make differential diagnoses. In addition, they want to be able to share information about diagnosis with those clients who want it, and they want to do so in a way consistent with enhancing strengths and resources. In conversation with other professionals, the therapist wants to convey understanding of diagnosis while simultaneously communicating the solution-focused and strategic attitude that diagnosis may not be the most interesting thing about clients. One creative way of doing this was suggested by Gorden (2010a), who described ways of looking for "stories of hope" (p. 168) in each criterion of the *DSM* borderline personality disorder diagnosis.

SPEAKING THE LANGUAGE OF THE SYSTEM

The larger systems in which solution-focused and strategic therapists practice often have other assessment procedures or requirements that may not seem to be directly related to solution-focused or strategic assessment. For example, an agency or managed care reviewers may ask therapists to conduct a formal mental status exam or take a more detailed developmental history. Sometimes that information is collected on an intake questionnaire and reviewed with the client as needed during the session. Ideally, such a form asks about strengths and victories as well as symptoms and problems, but even if it does not, skilled solution-focused and strategic therapists can use the information in ways that highlight resilience and convey respect for both the client and the system. Or therapists may be able to collect most of the information needed using their solution-focused and strategic tools. When additional information is required, the therapist can openly acknowledge that the agency wants some additional information. Clients deal with multiple systems too, and they understand the need to follow procedures. All information can be received through the kind of extreme listening described earlier, and this increases the likelihood that it may be useful in an unanticipated way, becoming an ingredient of a future solution.

6

Developing a Case Conceptualization and Intervention Plan in the Solution-Focused and Strategic Therapies

This chapter addresses how solution-focused and strategic therapists approach three of the core competencies that are part of a larger "intervention planning domain": clinical case conceptualization, treatment planning, and creating an integrative clinical case report. As discussed in previous chapters, the strategic solution focused therapist working with a new client has collected the following information: the client's view of the problem, the client's best hopes and worst fears, the client's readiness for change, the client's strengths, systemic variables, the client's view of a preferred future, pieces of the solution that are already happening, and solutions previously attempted both by the client and by others. Now it is time for the therapist to put all of this information together, in an integrative conceptualization of the case. From that case conceptualization will grow a treatment plan, tailored to this client's unique situation and designed to amplify what works and to change what does not. All of the above can then become part of a clinical report that captures the content and process of the interaction, simultaneously reflecting the attitudes of solution-focused and strategic therapy and providing documentation appropriate for the therapist's practice setting.

CASE CONCEPTUALIZATION IN GENERAL

Case conceptualization has been described as a way of summarizing and organizing seemingly diverse information into a map that elucidates and guides the treatment process (Sperry, 2010b). This includes looking at precipitants and recognizing that similar symptoms may result from different, sometimes opposite, situational factors. In Sperry's example, for one person, failure to receive a promotion at work results in depression, whereas for another, *getting* a promotion leads to depression. Complaints that on the surface seem to be the same may require very different treatment plans. Therapists vary in their levels of proficiency in case conceptualization. Sperry (2010a) noted that highly competent therapists ask "What, why, and what can be done about it?" Somewhat less competent therapists attempt to consider those variables, but their plans may be less clearly tailored to individual needs, and therapists at the beginning levels of competency may think they are doing case conceptualization but may simply be describing or repeating what the client said in a session (Sperry, 2010a).

Sperry (2010a) has commented that during case conceptualization, the therapist can function as an investigator, travel planner, or forecaster. As a forecaster, one role of the therapist is to predict obstacles that might interfere with treatment. This is, of course, one part of forecasting. However, a solution-focused therapist might focus on another kind of forecasting: predicting solutions, including places where change may emerge first, in view of this client's unique combination of interests, resources, and activities of daily life. There might also be forecasting of metaphors likely to resonate with this person, ways of joining with him or her.

MODALITY, NUMBER, AND FREQUENCY OF SESSIONS

Will treatment be in individual sessions, or will couple, family, or group sessions be part of the plan? Will the plan include medication (and referral to a provider who can prescribe, if the therapist cannot do so)? Will the number of sessions and intervals between sessions (weekly, every other week) be decided at the beginning of treatment or determined session by session? Solution-focused and strategic therapists discuss these questions with their clients, offering resources available in the practice or the community and tailoring the plan to client needs and preferences.

In some models of therapy, a first session is almost always an "intake," with the "real work" of therapy taking place in subsequent appointments. Solution-focused and strategic therapists know that this is not always the case. Whether by design or otherwise, the most frequent number of sessions with a therapist (statistically, the modal number of sessions) is *one*, according to some statistics (Miller, Norcross, Polster, & Prochaska, 2008). Some clients may prefer or expect a one-time consultation. In integrated healthcare, solution-focused and strategic therapy consultations in medical care settings, with feedback to other healthcare providers, are a variation of single-session therapy. Here, the plan may be follow-up with a medical care provider.

The Mental Research Institute (MRI) team has used an "up to 10 sessions" model, but when complaints appear to be resolving sooner, the therapist often suggests "keeping the remaining sessions in the bank." Considering "how brief is brief [therapy]?" de Shazer (as cited in D. Simon, 1993, p. 1) responded: "Not one session more than necessary." It is often extremely difficult to predict in advance how many sessions will be needed. Although solution-focused and strategic therapies are typically brief, this is not always the case. Solution-focused and strategic approaches work well in intermittent care and with clients who have been diagnosed with chronic symptoms. Determining how many sessions will be scheduled is discussed further in Chapters 8 and 9.

THE CLIENT AS COLLABORATOR IN CONCEPTUALIZATION AND TREATMENT PLANNING

For solution-focused and strategic therapists, the process of combining and integrating information takes into account the multiple variables described so far in this book. As noted, the nature of the complaint, how it is a problem, who is the customer, the client's readiness for change, the client's strengths, systemic variables, any attempted solutions that have not worked well enough, the client's view of a preferred future, and pieces of the solution that are already happening are all considered. Another extremely important variable to be considered is the client's view of both the problem and the solution. The client's "theory of therapy" is consistently addressed in the solution-focused and strategic approaches, by the strategic therapist's concept of client "position" and by inquiry about best hopes and best and worst messages.

Many therapy models use homework, and usually the homework is suggested by the therapist. In solution-focused and strategic solution focused sessions, therapists suggest homework too, but the experiment or homework more often grows from what the client either has suggested or is already doing. There is an assumption that what comes from the client is better than what comes from the therapist. In part this is because it is familiar and already part of the client's behavioral repertoire. de Shazer and Dolan (2007) pointed out that things that are foreign and unfamiliar take more work to accomplish—and therefore may result in what other models may call *resistance*. They wrote, "Creating [one's] own homework assignments reduces [one's] natural tendency to resist outside intervention, no matter how good the intention" (p. 11). The therapist can directly ask the client, "If you were to give yourself a homework assignment, what might it be?" The homework projects suggested are frequently creative things that neither therapist nor client could have predicted beforehand.

In the book *Therapy With "Impossible" Cases*, Duncan, Hubble, and Miller (1997) reminded readers that children as well as adults need to be asked what they think will help. They described a child diagnosed with separation anxiety disorder who had trouble sleeping in her own room. By age 10, she was already considered an "impossible case." After she was doing better, her therapist asked her what she thought had made the difference. She answered,

> I feel a lot better now that I came up with the solution to sleep in my own room, and I did it, and I'm proud of myself. And I couldn't be proud of myself if you told me, "How about if you barricade yourself in with pillows, maybe that'll work?" I wouldn't feel like I've done it. So basically, what I'm saying is you don't get as much joy out of doing something when somebody told you to do it. (Duncan et al., 1997, as cited in Duncan, 2010, p. 91)

This is an example of how an attitude, a client-directed stance of leading from behind, was crucial. In this case it was not just the suggestion but the fact that it came from the client that made a difference.

Best hopes inquiry, introduced in previous chapters, involves the client in both case conceptualization and treatment planning. The following example illustrates how the client's best hopes influenced the treatment plan.

Therapist: So, what are your best hopes from coming here?

Mary: Well, I'm depressed.

Therapist: And if coming here helps you with that, how will you know?

Mary: Well, I guess I'd feel better.

Therapist: Really, tell me more about that.

Mary: More energy, maybe. I wouldn't feel like everything sucks. Life won't feel so heavy.

Therapist: And how will that show?

Mary: Well, I might pick up the crap on the bedroom floor. There's got to be three weeks of laundry there.

Therapist: Dirty or clean?

Mary: Oh, it's clean.

Therapist: Really? Just needs to be put away?

Mary: Yeah, just need to get off my you know what and do it.

Therapist: Hmm. What else will be different when life isn't so heavy?

Mary: Well, I might put on makeup in the morning. Well, actually I put it on today, but that's just because I was coming here.

Therapist: Really? [Pause] Hey, Mary, if I had the privilege of knowing you really well, over time, over many years, what really special thing would I know about you, that might not be immediately obvious? It's okay to guess.

Mary: I have this weird sense of humor. I mean, not much lately, maybe, but I used to be able to take just about anything and turn it into a bad joke.

Therapist: What's the worst thing I could be saying to you or recommending today? What would make you go—Yuck, they told me I should go and talk to a therapist, and then that clown goes and tells me this?

Mary: Probably that I have to take medicine. That's what everyone says. You're depressed: Take drugs, best thing since sliced bread.

Therapist: And what's the opposite of that? What's the best thing I might
     say, that would make you feel that you got exactly what you
     wanted and needed today?
Mary: That you can help me. That I'm not going to feel like crap forever.
     That there's something I can do about it.

When asked at the end of the session what she wanted to remember from
today, Mary said, "I did put makeup on today. And that I can do it again,
sometimes. I don't have to do it every day. And that the laundry on the
floor is clean. It's not three loads of dirty laundry on my bedroom floor.
And that you didn't tell me I had to take drugs. There's a class I can go to."

     Here is how this might be written in a short note, and/or in an "after
visit summary" (a short document given to the client in some settings):

Goals: Decrease depression.
Short-term goals: Put away laundry. Wear makeup sometimes.
Treatment plan: Depression group, to begin in 2 weeks. Individual
     therapy, with next appointment in one week and number and fre-
     quency of sessions to be determined.

The reader is now invited to consider how the treatment plan—and the
documentation—would shift if Mary gave the following response to the
"worst and best message" questions. Here is the worst message: "That
I have to go to some group. I'm not going to talk about personal things
in front of other people and, frankly, I don't want to hear other people's
problems." Here is the best: "That you're going to give me some medicine,
and it's going to help me with this." What she wants to remember in this
variation is this: "You heard me. That you said I'm doing the right thing
by coming here, and that medicine can help me. And I'm actually kind
of intrigued by what you said about how I didn't have to wait to start the
medicine in order to put on makeup today. And that I can put the laundry
away before I see the doctor. And that it might start getting easier to do
that stuff once the medicine kicks in."

     In this variation, here is the documentation:

Goals: Decrease depression.
Short term goals: Put away laundry. Wear makeup sometimes.
Treatment plan: Medication evaluation with psychiatrist in one
     week. Individual therapy, with next appointment in one week and
     number and frequency of sessions to be determined.

84

ANTICIPATING OBSTACLES AND
PLANNING TO ADDRESS THEM

As noted in Chapters 3 and 4, obstacles to treatment can include relationship factors and reactions that come from both the client and the therapist. In addition, obstacles can take the form of limited availability of appointments. The fee or cost sharing (copay), insurance coverage, the availability of groups (Do they meet at a time the client can attend?), and transportation issues can all interfere with treatment. Some people will not come to a building that is called "mental health clinic" or for "counseling" or to see a "psychologist," but they will talk to "the internist's colleague" housed in a primary care setting. The solution-focused and strategic therapies are ideally suited for use in integrated healthcare, because intervention as well as assessment routinely occurs during a first appointment.

Anticipating obstacles, one of the competencies in case conceptualization, can be built into solution elaboration. This is routinely done by strategic solution focused therapists in the common variation of the miracle question that asks about slips and recovery. In this variation, at some point during the solution elaboration process, the therapist might say, "Imagine that, as more days go by, these changes build, and grow. And then one day you slip a little, and the problem starts to come back. What will be different about how you get back on track sooner, as a result of all these good changes you've just described?"

WRITING THE CLINICAL REPORT

Clinical records serve multiple functions. They provide a roadmap for treatment, they document requests for service and referral, and they describe the course of treatment and termination. They offer continuity of care when multiple providers work with clients. Some kind of documentation is typically needed for insurance reimbursement, managed care panels, and institutional utilization review. Records vary in the level of detail included, with "psychotherapy records" sometimes seen as different from general clinical records.

Sperry (2010b) asserted that the clinical report should not just state facts or summarize what the client said. He recommended that the report should include explanatory factors and ideas about treatment. It should be tailored to the individual. It should be internally consistent and sufficiently descriptive and compelling that another clinician could "pick the client out of a line up." As therapists' skills grow, their treatment plans and reports increasingly meet these criteria.

Who will see the report? Will it be appropriate for the client to view, if he or she wishes? Sometimes records are shared with clients who request them; sometimes therapists prepare summaries. Because most solution-focused and strategic solution focused therapists are transparent about their work, they will generally be comfortable sharing whatever is written with the client. Some strategic therapists might prefer that the client not see a clinical report that describes how an intervention was planned to reverse a particular attempted solution or to tap into a particular position variable. However, that is not always the case. Paul Watzlawick described working with a client who said, "I know all about your approach. You can't use it on me." Watzlawick told him, "Marvelous! Then our work should go even faster!" (Watzlawick, 1992).

Reports need to be tailored to the setting in which the therapist practices. A report written for other solution-focused and strategic therapists may not always include a full developmental history or multiaxial diagnosis, as noted in Chapter 5, but if a therapist practices in a setting that requires those things, that information needs to be part of the report.

Sperry (2010b) noted that sometimes therapists tend to write identical or almost identical treatment plans for almost every client they see. This might be more likely for a therapist at the lower levels of proficiency. In the solution-focused and strategic therapies, the detail elicited about complaints, solutions, exceptions, and attempted solutions makes it possible for even developing therapists (at the advanced beginner level and beyond) to incorporate some of that detail in their treatment plans. At higher levels of proficiency, therapists become increasingly skilled at incorporating that detail into the end-of-session input—and into the case report or clinical record.

When the client is a couple or family, the question arises of whether a note or report is written for the interpersonal system as a whole or for each individual. Often the report is richer and more complete when it describes the whole couple or family, but sometimes institutional policies require separate individual notes. Therapists at higher levels of proficiency are more likely to be able to describe systemic issues (such as attempted solutions or miracles that include multiple people) in a note that can be part of the record for each individual, with additional information about individuals as needed.

Writing a clinical report is sometimes seen as something done primarily after intake and perhaps at termination as well. However, in many settings, therapists are asked to produce documentation of some kind after every session. The focus, progress toward the goal, and the current goals all need to be described. At the higher levels of proficiency, the therapist uses the detail from that session in the documentation, weaving together new information with past themes, strengths, and solutions known from the past.

In many settings, reports become part of the electronic medical record, and this practice is likely to increase in the near future. Therapists can develop computer tools, including "smart phrases" that remind them to include client best hopes, solution scenarios, and attempted solutions in their documentation. These tools help to keep documentation solution-focused and strategic, and they also remind other providers who read the notes to routinely consider these variables in their clinical work.

CARMEN: CASE CONCEPTUALIZATION AND INTERVENTION PLANNING

The next section describes strategic solution focused case conceptualization and treatment planning with Carmen, the client introduced in Chapter 5. It might be noted here that in clinical case conceptualization, as with most things, the quality of the finished product is highly dependent on the quality of the ingredients that go into it. If certain pieces of information are not available, even a highly skilled therapist will be at a disadvantage. (Or he or she might recognize that this is a good time for a skeleton key intervention, something discussed in more detail below and in the following chapter.)

At higher levels of competency, solution-focused and strategic therapists will use their *knowledge* of the model, their *attitudes* of "extreme listening" and focusing on strengths more than on pathology, and their *procedures* for using solution-focused and strategic inquiry. Therefore, they will, for the most part, have "high-quality raw ingredients" to work with. That is, they are likely to have details about the presenting complaint, why now, and who is the customer; they will know something about the client's position and theory of change; and they may have rich detail about what the solution will look like, ideally with scaling numbers and information about pieces of the solution that are already happening. They may have learned about attempted solutions, successful and unsuccessful.

We will assume that all of the information about Carmen described in the previous chapter is available and that it is now time to conceptualize the case and to develop an intervention for her. For the purposes of this discussion, we will also imagine that this session has been done in front of a one-way mirror (as done at the Mental Research Institute [MRI], the Brief Family Therapy Center [BFTC], and in some training settings) and that the therapist has taken a short break and is consulting with solution-focused and strategic colleagues. We will imagine how a group of highly proficient strategic solution focused therapists would proceed.

What variables will the therapists consider? As Quick (2008) has suggested, they will look at the complaint and "why now?" They will consider Carmen's best hopes and worst fears and any unique ways of cooperating. They will consider her readiness for change, because this makes a difference for the kind of intervention that might be indicated. If Carmen appears to be a customer, she might be a candidate for behavioral homework of some kind, whereas if she is more of a complainant, a suggestion for observation might be indicated. And if she is primarily a visitor, there at someone else's request, it might be more appropriate to thank her for coming and to invite her to return in the future if she wishes.

The therapists will look at Carmen's capacity to describe a preferred future and the level of detail given, and they will assess whether pieces of the solution are already happening. They will consider solutions attempted, successful and unsuccessful. They will ask: Will it be more helpful to invite this client to amplify pieces of the solution, reverse any unsuccessful attempted solutions—or both? Will the input be specific or generic? (Quick, 2008). They will recognize that specific input is preferable, when possible, but that when it is not clear what to suggest, "skeleton key" interventions can be designed both to build on solutions and to invite something different. If the therapists have different ideas about what to suggest, they might consider a "split team" intervention (Quick, 2008), where the therapist tells the client that different colleagues had different ideas—and then presents all of them. The therapists will consider Carmen's special qualities, cultural background, and interests—her "position"—in deciding how to present any input. If there is a component that may seem counterintuitive, they will consider how to introduce it.

With all of these things in mind, the therapists will consider Carmen. First they will look at what is known about the complaint. Carmen has described multiple concerns, including financial concerns; marital conflict; difficulties managing tearfulness; impatience (yelling at her husband, mother, and son); sleep and appetite disturbance (increased appetite and both increased and decreased sleep); feelings of depression, guilt, and anxiety (which she calls "worry"); and concern about her special needs son. The reactions that Carmen describes have been present for about 3 weeks. The precipitant for her request for an appointment was a surge in feelings of guilt, in response to the possibility of her homeless mother moving in, with her husband not immediately rejecting the idea and her father's messages of "Just set limits" and "Don't feel guilty." Carmen felt internal conflict, sometimes "sneaking" her mother in for a shower and then hiding the fact that she had done this from her husband. Carmen's highest priority complaint is the concern about her mother and how she is responding to her, both in terms of her behavior (yelling, inconsistency) and her feelings (guilt). Assuming that Carmen is the expert about what concerns her most, the therapists will focus primarily on Carmen's reactions to her mother.

Next, the hypothetical treatment team will look at what emerged during the solution elaboration phase of the session. They will consider Carmen's best hopes and worst fears: What does she want, and how does she hope that therapy will help? Has she said or implied that change will grow from some particular component of treatment, such as medication, advice, opportunity to ventilate, insight, or some combination of these things? Was she able to envision and describe a preferred future in specific detail, building on therapist suggestions? If the solution inquiry included coping with obstacles and setbacks, was she able to imagine moving beyond them, in a "miracle" that is not just a "Pollyanna" picture of a world where nothing goes wrong? Are pieces of her solution already happening? Was she able to use scaling and to describe a next step in the right direction? What strengths are evident, and which does she notice and value most? Was she able to connect with the therapist? Did she indicate that she felt a bond with the therapist?

In this case, Carmen participated actively in solution elaboration. She clearly said what she wanted: suggestions about how to talk to Mom— and that leaving the session *without* some guidelines about that would leave her dissatisfied. In response to miracle question inquiry, Carmen elaborated a detailed picture that included dialogue and behavioral detail of how she would respond differently to her mother, husband, and son.

She described ways of responding to obstacles, such as Mom showing up at her door. She came up with her own creative suggestion (saying "No" to Mom for today but suggesting an alternate time to get together at the park). This combination of limit setting with reaching out has the capacity to diminish the guilt that Carmen finds so painful, while simultaneously allowing her to maintain boundaries at home. Carmen responded to scaling question inquiry, and she said that discussing her plan "in here" felt like part of her solution was beginning to happen.

Carmen displayed multiple strengths. She responded to the therapist in an easy, conversational way, building on therapist input. She clearly cares about her family members. She maintains a steady job and cares for a son with special needs. She wants to improve her marriage and decrease her irritability with her husband. She is open to suggestions, actively requesting them, and at the same time is able to create an idea that fits into the context of her routine. Carmen recognizes that she likes to figure things out and understand things. She is proud of her determination and her decision not to drink alcohol.

Expert strategic solution focused therapists will also consider what else is known about Carmen, either from the interview or from agency forms that she has completed. It is known that Carmen is an only child, with a high school education. She was born in the United States; her parents moved from Guadalajara, Mexico, to California before she was born. Carmen describes herself as second-generation Hispanic; she speaks both Spanish and English and is quite fluent in English. Her son calls Carmen's mother "Lita" (short for *abuelita*, "grandmother" in Spanish). Carmen's husband is Caucasian. Carmen's parents divorced when she was 12; her father left because of the mother's drinking. Carmen continued to live with her mother and briefly attended Alateen meetings. She has not had previous therapy. She describes herself as overweight, without other medical conditions. She takes birth control pills. She has never taken medicine for depression, anxiety, or other psychological complaints, and she is not interested in doing so now. On her intake form, Carmen denied any thoughts of harming herself or anyone else, currently or in the past. She answered "Yes" to the question on the form about "verbal abuse" received in the past (from mother) but "No" to questions about any sexual or physical abuse received.

The expert strategic solution focused therapy team will next review attempted solutions. They will look at behaviors, things Carmen has actually done, and they will consider suggestions and messages, both those given by others and those that appear in her own self-talk. They will look for patterns and similarities between seemingly different attempts, and they will consider whether these solutions are working. In Carmen's case, they will see that Carmen has tried to "be consistent" and "not feel guilty." These messages come from her dad, her husband, and herself. There has also been a somewhat mixed message from her husband. On one hand, he recently suggested that Mom's moving in might not be terrible if it helped with babysitting expenses, but his main message appears to encourage Carmen to set a consistent boundary with Mom. These attempted solutions have not worked well enough, because Carmen is still yelling; she also sneaked Mom in for a shower without admitting it to her husband, and she still feels distressed, worried, and guilty.

With all of this information in mind, the therapists will plan end-of-session feedback for Carmen, with three components: validation, compliment, and suggestion/input. First, they will consider what they want to validate. The therapist will want to let Carmen know that her dilemma has been heard. It is not easy to balance one's caring and feelings of responsibility and concern, on the one hand, with the pressure she feels to maintain boundaries, on the other. In addition, anger and feelings about Mom's problem are not new. It makes sense that Carmen is feeling conflicted, and it makes sense that her yelling and sleeping and eating changes have happened when there was increased pressure because of Mom's homelessness.

The second part of the intervention will be the compliment component (although the therapist will not use the word *compliment* with the client). What will be highlighted? The therapists will include Carmen's caring about her family, including the "Ronnie–Lita relationship," her determination, the fact that she knows and can articulate what she wants (suggestions about what to say to Mom), her ability to describe so clearly what change will look like, and her recognition that Mom may be difficult and that she can deal with this. Most of all, the therapist will point out that Carmen has created an idea for her own solution: the combination of limit setting with the invitation for a park visit.

For the suggestion/input component, the therapists will need to decide whether they want to plan amplifying what works, interrupting what does not, or both. In this case, they will do both. Carmen can be invited to "make pieces of her miracle happen and notice how that makes a difference." In particular, she can be encouraged to implement her own idea about the limit setting and park visit.

Because "Just set consistent limits" and "Don't feel guilty" have not worked well enough, highly proficient strategic solution focused therapists will recognize that those messages might need to be interrupted. Considering what is known about Carmen and her position, they will remember that she "likes to understand things and think about them." Tapping into this strength, the therapist can present the philosophy of "doing what works and changing what does not" and discuss how commonsense ideas sometimes do not work well enough. Together the therapist and Carmen can brainstorm opposites of "Just set consistent limits" and "Don't feel guilty."

If Carmen would like some suggestions (and it is likely that she will, because this is what she has requested), the therapist might suggest *expecting* to be inconsistent at times—and perhaps to share with Zach that the therapist suggested this. The therapist might tell Carmen that there is a chapter in the strategic therapy literature entitled "OK—You've been a bad mother" (Weakland, 1978). In that chapter, the therapist suggests that a mother tell her daughter something like this: "If I were a better mother, I'd drive you to the mall. Sometimes I'm not as good a mother as I should be." For Carmen, the variation might be: "Mom, maybe if I were a better daughter, I'd let you stay with me. Sometimes I guess I'm not as good a daughter as I should be."

By the time all of this has been done, the clinical report has essentially been written. What has been described above essentially *is* the clinical report for a class or seminar on solution-focused and strategic therapy. However, if the report is being written for the clinical record in the therapist's practice (as opposed to being written for a class or clinical seminar on solution-focused and strategic therapy), some additional information required by the practice setting will be included. As described in Chapter 5, this might include diagnosis and health or developmental history detail, perhaps obtained through a questionnaire or during a part of the interview in which the therapist openly acknowledges that some information is needed for the record.

It may be useful to consider how a strategic solution focused therapist at a lower level of competency might conceptualize the situation, plan intervention, and document differently. Even if all of the information available here had been collected (and, as described above, a less proficient therapist might *not* have all this data), conceptualization and intervention planning might be less sophisticated. In considering the area for change, there might be more of a focus on "depression" in general, with less recognition of what Carmen has described as primary. The fact that Carmen wants suggestions—and that she has created her own amazing idea—might not be recognized or articulated. At lower levels of proficiency, a therapist might suggest "Just be consistent" and "Don't feel so guilty" because these things seem so reasonable, without recognizing that this input would be repeating unsuccessful attempted solutions. A less proficient therapist might not have the *knowledge* of the strategic therapy literature or the *attitude* of truly believing that Carmen can know what she wants and come up with her own solutions. That therapist might not know the *procedures* to use when introducing ideas for both building on what works and changing what does not. In the clinical report, a less competent therapist might not convey Carmen's special characteristics or describe them clearly enough for another clinician to understand or continue to highlight them. A solution-focused or strategic therapist who does not value diagnosis or background information might omit that information from the report, producing a document that does not meet the standards of the practice setting.

Here is an example of how this case might be documented in an electronic medical record, in a format that is required for first appointment documentation in the practice setting and also includes solution-focused and strategic information. Within the report, the sections required by the practice setting are indicated by CAPITALIZED ITALICS, and the subheadings added to include strategic solution focused information are indicated by *lowercase italics*.

INTAKE REPORT

IDENTIFYING INFORMATION: The client is a 28-year-old Hispanic, married woman, employed as a word processor in a county government office, mother of one son. She is self-referred, with a chief complaint of "depression." She was seen individually, and the session was conducted in English.

PRESENTING PROBLEM: The client describes 3 weeks of depression, with complaints of tearfulness, impatience (yelling at her husband, mother, and son), sleep and appetite disturbance (increased appetite and both increased and decreased sleep), and feelings of depression, guilt, and anxiety, which she calls "worry." She describes financial concerns, marital conflict, and difficulties managing her special needs son. Her mother, who has struggled with drinking for years, recently became homeless and has been calling the client "25 times a day." The client describes internal conflict, sometimes "sneaking" her mother in for a shower and then hiding the fact that she has done this from her husband. The client's highest priority complaint is the concern about her mother and how she is responding to her mother, both in terms of her behavior (yelling, inconsistency) and her feelings (guilt).

Why now: The precipitant for the request for an appointment was a surge in feelings of guilt, in response to the possibility of her homeless mother moving in, with her husband not immediately rejecting the idea.

Best hopes: "To know how to deal with Mom, to deal with stress better," which will be evident to client when she feels more relief, happiness, and patience, and less worry.

Worst message a therapist could give: "Not giving me any suggestions."

Best message a therapist could give: "Tangible words I can tell my mom, suggestions."

Solution elaboration: Client response to miracle question inquiry: Will tell Mom she cannot visit today. Husband will notice that she "means it," is less upset, with less nagging. She will ask less of him, "just rinse out his glass." Husband will joke more, and son will notice parents arguing less, watching television together. If Mom comes over, client will ask her to leave. If son asks why Lita (his grandmother) is crying, she will say that Lita was not feeling well, and that this was not a good day for them to play together. She will suggest an alternative, Saturday at the park. She describes setting further limits with Mom. On a 0–10 scale, where 10 is the miracle, she rates self at 6, as a result of "having a plan." "Actually doing it" will bring her to a 7.

Attempted solutions: Client's husband, father, and her own self-talk have suggested "Be consistent" and "Don't feel guilty." These messages have not worked well enough.

DEVELOPMENTAL/FAMILY INFORMATION: Client was born and raised in California, where parents moved from Guadalajara, Mexico, before she was born. She is an only child. Her mother has struggled with alcohol abuse for many years, and client reports that mother was sometimes "verbally abusive" when drinking but that there was no sexual or physical abuse. Her father divorced her mother when client was 12, and she continued to live with her mother, with ongoing contact with her father. She has been married for 6 years to Zach, who is Caucasian. They have a 5-year-old son, Ronnie, who has a mild hearing loss, hyperactivity, and who "screams." Ronnie is in child care in the neighborhood. Client considers herself Hispanic, speaks mostly English, and says that she has friends (Hispanic, Caucasian, and Black) at work and in the neighborhood. She considers her in-laws supportive. Her husband drives a delivery truck for a local business, which has had financial problems, and she considers her job more stable than his. Finances are a concern. She was raised Catholic, as was her husband, but they do not attend church regularly.

OCCUPATIONAL/EDUCATIONAL INFORMATION: Client has a high school diploma and works as a word processor for the county. She enjoys crafts and taking her son to the park.

Special thing about client: "I have a good head on my shoulders." Likes to understand and think about things; determination.

HEALTH INFORMATION, MEDICATIONS: Overweight. Birth control pills.

CLIENT PSYCHIATRIC HISTORY: No past treatment with either psychotherapy or medication. There may have been some untreated anxiety and depression at time of parents' divorce. Attended Alateen in adolescence.

FAMILY PSYCHIATRIC HISTORY: Mother has struggled with alcohol abuse for many years.

SUBSTANCE USE INFORMATION: None. (Client verbalizes active decision not to drink because of her mother's problems with alcohol.)

MENTAL STATUS: Appropriately and casually dressed, with a full and appropriate range of affect and behavior. She is fully oriented. Speech is logical and coherent. Cognitive functioning, judgment, insight, and perception appear to be intact.

SAFETY/RISK INFORMATION: There is no evidence of danger to self or others.

DIAGNOSIS:

AXIS I: Adjustment reaction with mixed anxiety and depressed mood; parent–child problem (relationship with mother); rule out marital problem.

AXIS II: Deferred.

AXIS III: Rule out mild obesity.

AXIS IV: Relationship (mother, husband) and financial stressors; stress of dealing with special needs son.

AXIS V, CURRENT GAF: 65; *HIGHEST GAF IN LAST YEAR:* 75.

GOALS: Decrease depression, tearfulness, irritability, internal conflict. Improve relationships with mother, husband, and son.

SHORT-TERM GOALS (BEHAVIORAL AND OBJECTIVE): Notice "pieces of the miracle" happening. Set limit with mother visiting *and* invite mother to park for time with son. Rinse out husband's glass. If opportunity arises, tell mother "Sometimes I'm not as good a daughter as I should be."

TREATMENT PLAN: Individual strategic solution focused therapy, with next session in 2 weeks, at client's request, and with number of sessions and intervals between sessions to be determined in response to client preferences and progress. The client understands that medication consultation, group therapy, couples therapy, and family therapy are available, and she declines these at this time. Feedback has been given validating client's feelings, complimenting her on her ideas and plan, and encouraging "doing what works and changing what does not." Specifically, one component of the plan is to encourage client to use her own creative idea with her mother. Another component is to help client to recognize that "Set limits consistently" and "Don't feel guilty" do not always work well enough. The plan includes normalization of inconsistent behavior and feelings of guilt, in view of her difficult situation. It also encourages direct discussion with her mother about her "imperfection" as a daughter.

What client wants to remember: "When Mom, calls, I can tell her 'No.' It's okay to say 'Not today.' It's normal to feel guilt sometimes, and that doesn't mean I can't set limits. I don't have to yell. I like it that I can ask her to go to the park and that I have a plan if she has a meltdown."

7

Implementing Solution-Focused and Strategic Methods and Interventions

This chapter covers the four competencies that are part of intervention implementation: establishing a treatment focus, maintaining the treatment focus, addressing treatment-interfering factors, and applying specific solution-focused and strategic procedures. It discusses how problem clarification and solution elaboration focus the work to the most important areas, and it addresses how highly competent therapists use variations of the basic tools to address obstacles when they arise. The chapter covers common unsuccessful attempted solutions in depression, anxiety, relationships, and longstanding personal patterns (personality disorders)—and some alternatives. There is discussion of how and when to incorporate didactic information, other methods, and other modalities into the process. The interventions selected are collaboratively tailored to each client's goals, needs, preferences, and style of learning, with emphasis on doing what works and the expectation that "one size will not fit all."

ESTABLISHING A FOCUS

As discussed throughout this book, the problem clarification process is a critical component of the strategic and strategic solution focused models. Best hopes inquiry performs a similar function for solution-focused (and strategic solution focused) therapists. As Krishnamurthy et al. (2004)

have noted, in psychotherapy in general there is not a rigid boundary between assessment and intervention. This is particularly true in the solution-focused and strategic therapies, where treatment is sometimes completed in the amount of time that a full assessment might take in some other models.

Clearly, problem clarification is simultaneously an assessment and intervention tool. Arlene complained about being too shy. She wanted companionship and friends but feared reaching out to people. When the therapist asked for an example of the problem, Arlene described her reluctance to call or text a friend who lived in a nearby city. She called this her shyness. What did she fear would happen if she contacted her friend? Arlene said, "She'll ask me to go up there for an entire weekend, and I'll end up having to pay for both of us when we go out." This information narrowed the focus, leading to solutions involving limit setting and assertiveness for Arlene.

"Presuppositional questioning," described by O'Hanlon and Weiner-Davis (1989), influences clients during the information-gathering process. For example, a client describes two complaints: hearing voices and his wife's concern about the voices. The therapist asks him which of those things distresses him more: the voices or the wife's concern. This question implies that the voices (in and of themselves) might not be such a problem if the wife's concern were to diminish. The idea that the voices, which are often automatically assumed to be a serious psychiatric symptom, might *not* be the primary problem may be novel—and healing. Similarly, asking *how* something is problematic introduces the notion that some behavior or interaction might be present without necessarily being a problem. When the client is describing intense emotion and the therapist asks what happened to elicit that feeling, the implicit message normalizes strong reactions (Quick, 2008). The therapist might attempt to communicate something like this: "I assume you have an absolutely legitimate reason for feeling as you do. I mean, you seem like a pretty reasonable person to me. I really want to understand, and I hope our conversation will be useful for you. So if it would be helpful to do so, please tell me what happened."

Best hopes inquiry (and the full solution elaboration process) also have both assessment and intervention functions. While eliciting information about a desired future, the questions invite detail and noticing pieces of the solution that are already happening. A focus has been created: continuing along the "road" that travels from where the client is now toward that desired future. Sometimes the focus emerges through full miracle question elaboration; on many other occasions, the process involves what O'Hanlon and Weiner-Davis (1989) called "little miracle questions" or "fast forward questions" (p. 106). The client's responses—which, as noted previously, are not always obviously or directly related to anyone's description of the problem—guide both the therapist and the client in the desired direction. The view of the future creates the focus, and it also suggests tasks for the present. That process builds hope, one of the critical ingredients in healing and one of the "common factors" associated with change in psychotherapy.

MAINTAINING THE FOCUS

Once the road to the future has been created, the next task is to facilitate travel along that road, at a pace that fits the client. Journeys to the destination can be compared to road trips: Some people drive through the night, with only brief pit stops; others explore back roads; and still others change their plans en route. Sperry (2010b) noted that clients sometimes "chase rabbits," shifting the conversation from the primary focus to every little event or development in their lives. This process can definitely distract both therapist and client from the primary issue. Neither therapists nor clients (most clients!) truly want to change direction with every up and down of everyday life. Leading from behind, the therapist needs to discover how he or she can best facilitate the trip. This involves balancing the focus on the original goal with other topics that the client might introduce. Sometimes the process might involve asking whether the therapist can best help by collaboratively noticing "rabbit chasing" and guiding back to the main road. Many clients appreciate this support. The all-important attitudinal factor discussed throughout this book is relevant here, because the strategic solution focused therapist recognizes that for some clients, rabbit hunts are an essential ingredient of the solution.

Some clients shift directions between sessions, bringing up something totally different from the goal set last time. How might the strategic solution focused therapist point this out, while simultaneously respecting the client's right to establish the direction? The therapist certainly will not say, "Sorry, we can't talk about that. It's not on our list of goals." But he or she probably does want to check on whether the area for change has shifted and whether the goal from last time is still important. Maybe a problem has been resolved and is not an issue any more! If the issue has not been resolved to the client's satisfaction, the therapist can choose to inquire where things stand with it.

Leaning a bit in the direction of staying on track with one issue, R. Fisch (personal communication, 1989, as cited in Quick, 2008, p. 26) cautioned clients about the "inadvisability of moving on to 'Problem Number Two' before 'Problem Number One' is resolved, lest 'Problem Number One' rear its ugly head again." But again, once this has been said, it is fully up to the client to decide.

It is legitimate to shift the focus. Not only is it legitimate, but sometimes it is important to do so, because the shift may lead to an area that is now more important. Goals and directions are not static; they evolve, and often the change occurs *as a result of* reflection during and after therapy sessions. Highly effective therapists are better able to recognize this phenomenon, and they directly discuss it with their clients. Often well before their therapists introduce the notion of "baby steps" on the road to change, clients begin with a smaller issue. They may need to discover for themselves that the therapist is safe to trust with important concerns. Once they learn that the therapist is trustworthy, they may bring up a different issue—sometimes one that is just as important as (or more important than) the initial one.

An example of this is seen in a videotaped session (Miller, 1999) where the client began by discussing the issue that "some people think I have trouble with decision making." At the very end of the session, he noted that he also might be a bit depressed. In the commentary after the session, the observing therapists wondered whether the emergence of the depression as an issue so late in the session reflected therapist error. Although that is one possible way of viewing things, the therapist noted that for this client, who built trust slowly in all relationships in his life, it made perfect sense that he needed to address decision making before bringing up depression.

To maintain the focus in a way that works for this client, solution-focused and strategic therapists often use the client's own metaphors and language. In Miller's (1999) case described above, the client mentioned possible plans to marry his girlfriend during a trip to Las Vegas the following year. On several occasions, the therapist inquired about things the client might do "on the way to Vegas."

In the case described in Chapter 3 of this book, Cindy described feeling like she had blinders on: "like I'm seeing through blinders, like all I see is—I've lost my home, financially ruined, and I don't feel well." Building on Cindy's language, the therapist used the blinders image to introduce solution elaboration:

Therapist: Cindy, can I ask you a strange question?

Cindy: Sure.

Therapist: I want to invite you to imagine that while you're sleeping tonight, a miracle happens. And the miracle is that you can take the blinders off. You wake up. It's tomorrow morning. What's the first thing that will be different, that will let you know that you're starting to see the big picture?

Cindy: Um, less perseverating on the negative aspects of the situation. I'd have more energy.

Therapist: And how will that show?

Cindy: Maybe I'd look forward to dealing with family and friends. I might look forward to picnics with the family, playing volleyball.

As solution elaboration continued, Cindy described increasingly rich detail about the "big picture." She would call her daughters and arrange something for Mother's Day. Which will she call first? "Suzi, she's the one I told, 'No, I don't want to do anything for Mother's Day.'" They might take Subway sandwiches to the park. Cindy will have something to think about that is positive: "Which jeans fit, games Angela and I can play—something fun and easy; maybe we'll take the big bouncy ball." Jay will notice her enthusiasm, her energy, her staying up past eight o'clock. "I'll be more like my old self. I'll have my list of things to accomplish."

When it is a work day, Cindy will think about what she might do after work and what they might have for dinner. "The blinders will be open a little wider." She will tell people at lunch something funny Jay or the kids said. After work, she still will be tired, but on her drive home, her body will relax. "It's a 45-minute drive, and I really do like my drive. It gives me time to think. I'll plan something for when I get home. Here's what I always do: I go straight into the bedroom, put my old sweats on, lie down, and then it's all over. I don't want to move for an hour. You have to drag me up to get dinner. But I won't do that."

What will Cindy do instead? She will put her purse and laptop down, grab a soda, and sit with Jay. They will chat, maybe decide to go for a walk before dinner. As the changes grow, the good things will continue, to the next day, and then to the next.

101

The therapist continued the language of the blinders to inquire about slips and recovery: After a slip, how might Cindy open the blinders again? "By conscious thoughts of how I opened them last time," Cindy said, "and by being around my family, going for a picnic, going home with a plan."

ADDRESSING OBSTACLES

As discussed in previous chapters, obstacles can and do emerge in psychotherapy, and solution-focused and strategic therapists need to be ready to identify and address them. Rifts in the relationship, issues in the treatment setting and the outside world, and clients' unique ways of cooperating all emerge during treatment. Clients' readiness for change shifts; customers lose motivation, and new issues emerge. Sometimes clients want something that therapists cannot provide. This might be a service (one client wanted her therapist to provide authorization for new breast implants), or it might be some less tangible thing, such as "certainty" or "a guarantee that I'm making the right decision." Here, the therapist can empathize with the client's wish and then directly acknowledge what therapy can and cannot do.

Therapist inquiry about "best and worst messages" actively invites clients to describe things that might interfere with effective treatment, and sometimes clients respond with something that the therapist *would* do or say (in the absence of being asked not to!). Seth answered the "worst message question" by describing a past therapist who said "I validate you" frequently. Seth found this irritating and condescending. Strategic solution focused therapy typically includes a validation component. When it was time to plan the end-of-session feedback, the therapist wondered to herself, "Hmm, what should I do about validation? I want to let Seth know I hear him. But he's just told me he doesn't like 'validation'! Now, I know I don't use that language—I don't just say 'I validate you' the way he said his other therapist did—but I need to be really careful here. Should I skip validation altogether with Seth? I *could* do that, but I don't really want to. I really do want to let him know that I understand what's been going on." The therapist then realized that it was the *word* ("validation") that Seth found objectionable, not the whole concept. Choosing to use other language, and picking a phrase Seth had used earlier in the session, she said, "It really sucks when…." At the end of the session, Seth indicated that the conversation had been helpful. The therapist was glad that she had the "worst message" information—and that she had still decided to include some kind of validation, tailored to Seth's language and preferences.

In strategic solution focused therapy, therapy typically begins with problem clarification, followed by solution elaboration, evaluation of attempted solutions, and concluding with some feedback. However, as Quick (2008) has pointed out, problem clarification does not always clarify, and miracle questions do not always create miracles. In fact, sometimes an answer to the miracle question actually echoes an unsuccessful attempted solution (Quick). When one tool is not working, in the spirit of the model's guiding principles, the therapist will recognize it, and therapists at higher levels of competence recognize it sooner. They can then use another component of the model, move to a "change slowly" position, and/or check with the client about what would be most helpful right now.

Knowing what to do when one's standard techniques are not working characterizes the higher levels of competence in solution-focused and strategic therapy. Megan's therapist was using the same kind of problem clarification and solution elaboration questions that he always used, usually with positive results. However, Megan was finding the questions irritating. She burst into tears of frustration: "I didn't come here to be interrogated. If I knew the answers to all these things, I wouldn't be here." A therapist at the lower levels of proficiency might feel stuck. He might think, "Hmm, I've been taught that when one part of the model isn't working, shift to another part, but problem clarification, solution elaboration, and attempted solutions *all* involve questioning."

The therapist quickly reviewed in his mind: "When in this session was Megan *not* this upset?" He remembered her response to one of the first questions he had asked, about her best hopes from coming here. She had said, "I want some answers, some ways to cope with stress at work." Megan's work was stressful, she was divorced, she had recently bought a condo, and because of her house payments, she felt trapped and unable to leave her stressful job. The therapist had not asked the "best and worst message question" yet. He decided to do so, wording it like this: "Hey, Megan, I know this is another question, but what's the worst thing I could be suggesting to you today, in addition to asking you so many questions?"

Megan answered, "Telling me I need to go back on medication. I've been on it, off and on, for years, and every time I come to a place like this, that's what they tell me." The best message would be "There are some answers, some tools, besides medication." The therapist noticed his own feelings of irritation, along with this thought: "Of course there are tools beyond

103

medication—I was just using some—and you didn't like that either!" (He made an active choice not to say that aloud.) Instead, he asked, "What kind of tools?" Megan wanted some ideas, some different perspectives.

The therapist thought, "Okay, enough questions. I'm going to try to give her some suggestions. This may not be what my colleagues would call solution-focused or strategic therapy, but suggestions are what Megan wants right now." He brought up the idea of seeing work as a place to go in order to get money, benefits, and not expecting to *enjoy* going there. He used an analogy likely to resonate with someone who has recently bought a condo: "It's like getting stuff for your house—you go to the hardware warehouse for paint and nails but to the fabric store for curtains." By the end of the session, Megan thanked the therapist. "This was really helpful," she said.

When the therapist processed the interaction with Megan with his consultation group, his colleagues asked him what he liked best about how he had handled the session, and they told him what they saw. They highlighted his flexibility, his willingness to shift gears, and his ability to respond to what the *client* needed and wanted (rather than following some rigid plan for running the session). These things reflect the most important skills and attitudes of the strategic solution focused philosophy: doing what works and changing what does not.

SOLUTION-FOCUSED AND STRATEGIC TOOLS: USING THEM AT HIGHER LEVELS OF COMPETENCE

Problem Clarification

In theory, problem clarification should be easy. The beginner might think: "You just ask the client what the main problem is." Therapists quickly discover that clients come with multiple concerns, that different members of a family or system are customers for different things, and that the therapist cannot assume that the label the client gives to a problem reveals the most important things about it. (The example of Arlene's "shyness," described earlier in this chapter, illustrates this.) As discussed in previous chapters, problem clarification involves eliciting behavioral descriptions of the complaint, why now, in what way something is a problem, and how the client hopes that therapy will help. And although clarity of the complaint and the goal makes focus easier, highly competent solution-focused and strategic therapists recognize that some clients not only *like* to chase rabbits—they *need* to chase rabbits. Complaining about or "touching" multiple concerns helps them. There is a joke about the client who entered the therapist's office and complained for 50 minutes. The therapist said, "Our time is up," and the client said, "Thank you. I feel so much better." This is obviously *not* what typically happens in the solution-focused and strategic therapies, but therapists need to be mindful of the fact that problem clarification does not work for everyone. Quick (2008) described a client for whom therapist attempts to define a focus were not working. This man's car had a bumper sticker that said "All who meander are not lost," a phrase that became an ingredient of the man's solution!

Solution Elaboration

Solution elaboration includes communicating an essential attitudinal component: truly *wanting* to hear about the client's desired future and *believing* that the client has the ability to imagine and describe this future, even in extremely difficult situations. This belief grows from hearing clients with really serious problems give good answers to miracle questions. Clients may say that they do not believe in miracles. One highly proficient therapist, Korman, offered this response: "Me neither. But is it okay to pretend for a while?" (Korman, as cited in de Shazer & Dolan, 2007, p. 42). Quite often the answer is yes.

At lower levels of proficiency, therapists may ask miracle questions in a somewhat rote manner: "What will you be doing that's different at 7 a.m.? And at 8 a.m.?" With increasing skill at following the client, they develop a sense of when to move to a slightly more distant future, when to ask what others will notice, and when to ask a question that grows from the evolving solution scenario. At the earlier stages of competency, therapists may also wonder how to respond when clients answer miracle questions with things that are impossible. Therapists with higher levels of proficiency are prepared for this. de Shazer and Dolan (2007) described a man who lost his hand in an industrial accident who answered the miracle question by saying that his arm would be back in place. The therapist (de Shazer) empathically responded "Sure"—and waited. After a long silence the man said, "I guess you mean something that could happen." de Shazer nodded. The man then described how he would get up and make breakfast with his one arm. There was no further discussion about getting the arm back (p. 40). Clients know that therapists do not bring back body parts

105

or the deceased; nor do they help people win the lottery. Acknowledging and validating the wish is usually followed by a focus on what is possible.

In the same way, people frequently describe miracles in which outside things and other people change. There are (at least) two ways the therapist can respond to this. One involves asking, "And if that did happen, how will you be different as a result?" Continuing inquiry can make it clear that the client's changes might be possible even if the other person does not change first. Or the therapist can clarify—as de Shazer did with a woman who continued to elaborate about how her ex-husband would be different with the children—"This is a miracle that only hits your house, not his" (de Shazer & Dolan, 2007, p. 50). This client then began to describe how she would be different.

Highly proficient therapists ask variations on the miracle question that follow and build on the client's language. Inviting Cindy to see her world without blinders is an example of this. The word *miracle* is not always included—and sometimes it is deliberately omitted, a point discussed in more detail in Chapter 10. "Coping questions" invite clients to recognize and amplify how they get through difficult times. As discussed throughout this book, strategic solution focused therapists often inquire about miracles that include slips and recovery, including those in which relationship patterns and "bumps on your personality" emerge—and are not deal breakers. This kind of solution inquiry is particularly useful with relationship dilemmas and with clients who have been given diagnoses of personality disorder.

Evaluation of Attempted Solutions

Evaluating attempted solutions and considering ways of reversing unsuccessful ones also become more sophisticated at higher levels of proficiency. Some attempted solutions appear frequently, and highly competent strategic and strategic solution focused therapists recognize them more quickly. Quick (2008) has described the following common patterns. In depression, when variations of "Cheer up" do not work well enough, an alternative may be permission to mourn. When "Calm down" becomes an unsuccessful attempted solution for anxiety, expecting and seeking out discomfort, uncertainty, and imperfection are counterintuitive but often useful alternatives. With unsuccessful promises to change longstanding patterns (made both to others and to oneself), there is this alternative: "I may *not* fully change." When pressure to "decide," again from both oneself and others, does not work well enough, an alternative may be permission for ambivalence and taking one's time.

There are multiple ways in which unsuccessful attempted solutions can be interrupted, and more proficient strategic and strategic solution focused therapists tailor their choices to the client. Segal (2001) gave the example of a client who is anxious about public speaking. His unsuccessful attempted solution is pressure on himself to "give this presentation perfectly." The man might be encouraged to announce to his audience that he is nervous, to make a mistake on purpose, or to invite audience participation and then ask the audience, "Where was I?" This experiment might be suggested in different ways: as a way of gathering data, as preparation for a true emergency, or as a way of reversing "what isn't working." Beginners or advanced beginners might learn a single strategy and/or rationale for anxiety and then use that combination with every anxious client. At higher levels of competency, the strategy and the rationale provided are selected to fit the client and might include elements never used before.

Armand was fearful of both formal public speaking and casual interaction with women. His biggest fear was "wetting himself," something that had happened once, years ago, causing terrible embarrassment. Multiple therapists had encouraged Armand to "relax" and "not worry about it"—attempted solutions that repeated his own unsuccessful message to himself. Armand's therapist considered what would be both different and relevant to Armand's deepest fears. Together Armand and the therapist discussed a plan for Armand to keep a glass or bottle of water nearby in any situation where he felt anxious. If needed, he could quickly spill water on his lap (and in a true emergency, on people nearby), and then he could profusely apologize. Armand discovered that sharpening his skill in unobtrusively toppling water bottles boosted his confidence immensely. He also soon confided in a female friend about his problem. His therapist reflected to a supervision group that he had never seen this task on any list of evidence-based treatments for social anxiety.

Feedback

As described in Chapter 6, designing the intervention includes letting clients know that they have been heard and tailoring input to client preferences and language. The intervention for Cindy validated her feelings, complimented her ability to describe "opening up the blinders," and invited her to make pieces of that scenario happen. It included a gentle but specific "nudge" to call her daughter Suzi about a possible Mother's Day outing. The therapist also commented that when frustration or fatigue pulled the blinders on again (as they sometimes do), Cindy might use "conscious thoughts of how she opened the blinders before" (Cindy's own words). This intervention could not have been designed from knowledge of Cindy's complaints (frustration with work, fatigue, finances, and her husband) alone. Nor could its details have been predicted simply from knowing the therapist's model. It grew from a conversation guided by the model, followed by inviting the solution Cindy had created in the session. As noted previously, therapy is a collaborative process. It is like a dance: The therapist leads and also follows (Storm, 1991).

Here is an example where the therapist's input could not have been predicted from simply knowing the client's diagnosis. Duncan (2010) described a young man named Peter. Peter was terrorized by voices that told him that people were trying to kill him. To protect himself, Peter did things (such as perching on a road overpass with an empty rifle) that led to multiple hospitalizations and medications that brought tardive dyskinesia and 100 pounds of extra weight. Duncan wrote:

> Only because I had no clue about what to do, I asked Peter what he thought it would take to get a little relief from his situation. … After a long pause, Peter said something very curious—he said that it would help if he would start riding his bike again. This led to my inquiry about the word "again." Peter told me about what his life had been like before the bottom fell out. Peter had been quite the competitive cyclist in college and was physically fit as only world class cyclists can be. I heard the story of a young man away from home for the first time, overwhelmed by life, training day and night to keep his spot on the racing team and topped off by falling in love for the first time. When the inevitable came to pass and the relationship ended, it was too much for Peter, and he was hospitalized, and then hospitalized again, then hospitalized again, and so on until there was no more money or insurance—then the state hospitalization cycles ensued. (p. 31)

Treatment took Peter to a bike shop and eventually back to cycling, a bike club, and a supervised living arrangement. As Duncan pointed out, "You can read a lot of books about schizophrenia and its treatment, but you'll never find one that recommends biking as a cure" (p. 32).

Whatever the intervention delivered, therapists ideally provide it in language that fits with who *they* are (in addition to being tailored to client language). Some beginning solution-focused therapists make so much of an effort to echo the "Wow!" exclamation that Berg used that they sound forced or artificial. As competence grows, therapists discover their own voices.

Whenever possible, the language in therapist feedback is specific, with behavioral detail, often client generated. When it is not clear what detail would be helpful, the therapist may decide to offer a "skeleton key" intervention. As described by de Shazer (1988), some interventions are like skeleton keys, which can open multiple doors. Here are some examples of skeleton key goals and interventions:

- Between now and next time we get together, notice something in your life you would like to continue.
- Slip and get back on track.
- Write down 10 changes you'd like to see in your partner. Now write down 20 changes your partner would see in you if he or she made those changes.
- Do one thing differently—and notice how it makes a difference.
- Have a moment of discomfort—physical, psychological, or what-ever—and notice how you ride through it.

At higher levels of proficiency, therapists can more easily recognize when a skeleton key suggestion might be most helpful.

One component of strategic solution focused therapy is the balance between suggestions (both specific and skeleton key) that lean toward acceptance and those that lean toward change. Quick (2008) proposed that:

> ... the balance between stability and acceptance, on one hand, and change, on the other, occurs at several levels. The cycle occurs within the individual: People want change, and they want things to stay the same. Sometimes the feelings occur simultaneously (ambivalence), and sometimes feelings occur sequentially. The urge for stability commonly follows a change spurt—and vice versa. Does this client need a little "push" out of inertia? Or would "permission"—to take one's time, to change slowly—be more helpful right now? Or might the most helpful message include both components? (This is often the case.) ... There is also continual shifting within a course of therapy. Sometimes it occurs within a session, while sometimes it happens between sessions. (p. 213)

Linehan (1993) and Quick (2008) have both described how the dialectic between acceptance and change occurs for many clinical problems. As Quick put it:

The feeling or belief that "I must change this; I must eradicate this" becomes the unsuccessful attempted solution with multiple symptoms, in interpersonal problems, and in longstanding interpersonal problems (often referred to as personality disorders). Acceptance—of the fact that some difficulty will happen again—and that it does not have to become a "deal breaker"—often becomes the most elegant alternative. It can lead to the perspective that the client can ride through it (whatever "it" is), let go of it sooner, and do something different. ... Some of that process is often already happening and can be amplified. This, at the deepest level, is what strategic solution focused therapy is all about: doing more of what works, changing what does not, and noticing how those processes make a difference. (p. 215)

ADDING OTHER TOOLS TO STRATEGIC SOLUTION FOCUSED THERAPY

The reader of this book knows that problem clarification, solution elaboration, amplifying what works, and changing what does not are the primary methods in the solution-focused and strategic therapies. A flexible strategic solution focused approach can include other components as well. Many solution-focused and strategic therapists take delight in discovering new ideas, tools, and images to add to someone's solution. Sometimes a story, method, or perspective from another approach offers exactly what the client is requesting. On other occasions, the primary methods do not seem to be working well enough. In the spirit of doing what works, if the therapist knows that a particular tool exists, he or she might ask whether the client would like to know about it. Any ideas or suggestions are introduced respectfully and collaboratively, with the attitude that clients will use, adapt, or discard information in a way that works for them.

Some readers might wonder: Is offering suggestions consistent with the solution-focused emphasis on "leading from behind"? Terry Trepper described asking Berg what she thought about using specific sex therapy exercises in combination with solution-focused work (Trepper, Treyger, & Yalowitzh, 2007). Should one *not* introduce this information? Trepper stated that Berg responded, "Just because you're doing solution focused brief therapy, it doesn't mean you get stupid." In this spirit, didactic information, metaphors, group and class referral, and tools from other approaches may all become ingredients of the solution for some people. Working from a strategic solution-focused base, the author has sometimes added methods from dialectical behavior therapy, acceptance and commitment therapy, cognitive therapy, hypnosis, and mindfulness. As Trepper et al. emphasized, therapists do not suddenly take an expert stance, and they do not arbitrarily assign homework. They simply ask whether the client would like this information and, if so, they introduce it as a perspective that others have found useful, with an invitation to experiment with it and to be curious about what one might discover.

It might be noted that for some clients, psychotropic medication is one component of the solution. Some clients who come to therapists are already taking medication; they do not ask their therapists' opinion of it. As Quick (2008) pointed out, taking medication can be considered an attempted solution, sometimes a successful one and sometimes an unsuccessful one. When the client is not taking medication, many solution-focused and strategic therapists lean toward beginning therapy without medicine, in the spirit of doing the most straightforward thing first. If that does not work well enough, adding medication is one way of doing something different. It might be noted that for therapists who prescribe, the same philosophy applies to when to change the medicine or dose or to suggest therapy without medication: If it is not working well enough, do something different.

As discussed in Chapter 3, common factors (client factors, the relationship, and expectancy of positive change, or hope) have been said to account for as much of 85% of the change in psychotherapy (Lambert, 1992). Quick (2010b) has suggested that a "doing what works" approach to therapy may create and enhance the common factors. Strategic and solution-focused therapists tailor their work to unique client styles and preferences. They join with their clients and build strong relationships. They rapidly help clients to discover that pieces of their solutions may already be happening, a process that strengthens hope. Sometimes these processes produce change in and of themselves. When more is needed, they provide a solid base to which other methods can be added. In this sense, doing what works and changing what does not can become a transtheoretical philosophy (Quick, 2008), used by any psychotherapist, regardless of theoretical orientation.

8

Monitoring and Evaluating Clinical Outcomes

Psychotherapy outcome research shows that change early in treatment and client ratings of the therapeutic alliance are associated with positive outcomes, so solution-focused and strategic therapists clearly want to know what is working. They also want to know when treatment is *not* working well enough, so that, in the spirit of the model, they can "do something different." This chapter describes multiple ways in which solution-focused and strategic therapists routinely monitor client progress and modify treatment accordingly: one of the core competencies associated with intervention evaluation and termination. Sessions often begin with "What's better or different?" inquiry, which simultaneously monitors progress, highlights positive change, and guides the focus to areas of concern. Scaling questions, with endpoints anchored in the client's own language whenever possible, provide repeated measures of multiple variables. Solution-focused and strategic therapists may also use rating scales, both paper-and-pencil and computer based, that measure progress toward goals and clients' perceptions of the therapeutic alliance. Case examples illustrate how solution-focused and strategic therapists use the information obtained to tailor treatment to individual client needs.

PRACTICE-BASED EVIDENCE

As discussed in more detail in Chapter 11, experience is one "ingredient of the solution" in therapist competency, but it is clearly not the only one, and by itself, it is not sufficient. The common saying "practice makes perfect" is not really accurate; rather, "practice makes permanent" (Quick, 2008, p. 57). Therapists may use the same tools and respond in the same way for many years, increasing the "habit strength" of their responses—both those that are helpful to clients and those that are not. In addition, because "nothing works for everyone," as Norcross (2005) has noted, a therapist who uses exactly the same methods, in the same way, with every client, is guaranteed to do something that is not working with some of them.

As Duncan (2010) pointed out, all therapists have some clients with whom they are not effective. What discriminates highly effective therapists is that they discover this more quickly. Because they have the *knowledge* about this phenomenon, the *procedures* to elicit this information, and an *attitude* of eagerness to find out, they can nondefensively discover what is working and what is not. Sometimes, even in the presence of a strong therapeutic alliance, the client's symptoms are not changing. When this occurs, it is time to "do something different." This might include discontinuation of therapy, referral to a different therapist or community resource, or a different treatment method.

Sperry (2010b) has commented that therapists of the 21st century need to do more than provide effective treatment. They also need to be able to *demonstrate* that the treatment was effective. In the United States, this competency has become increasingly important since national healthcare reform has become a reality. One way of demonstrating effectiveness is through outcome studies. This book has already mentioned the psychotherapy outcome research documenting that common factors and specific techniques have both been associated with positive change. This is commonly referred to as *evidence-based practice*. There is another dimension as well. Sperry described it like this:

> The other perspective emphasizes "practice-based evidence," which is based on the premise that effectiveness is more a function of therapist–client collaboration than of specific treatment interventions. This second perspective places a premium on assessing specific treatment processes and outcomes measures, and requires therapists to monitor treatment processes and outcomes. (2010b, p. 241)

One way of monitoring both process and outcome involves simply assessing whether the client returned after a first (or most recent) visit. However, the meaning of returning—or not returning—is not always clear. Client return can be viewed as a reflection of at least adequate satisfaction with the treatment plan, progress, and/or the therapeutic alliance. It conveys that the client has not "dropped out" or terminated prematurely. But clients sometimes fail to return *not* because of premature termination but because their needs have been met. This phenomenon occurs in therapies of all orientations and is not unusual. Therapists may automatically assume that courses of treatment involve multiple visits, but clients may not. In healthcare settings and many other businesses, people frequently seek one-time consultations. In fact, Plante (2010) noted that one third of all psychotherapy clients are seen only one time. This statistic suggests that a large number of clients attend far fewer sessions than most therapists would predict.

In the solution-focused and strategic therapies, it can be a legitimate choice to leave it "open ended" after a visit, with the "door open" to return when and if it is desired. Although this plan is quite appropriate clinically, it sometimes makes it hard to know whether the session was helpful or not. For example, Nadia made an appointment to brainstorm ways of dealing with her mother. She said that she was satisfied with the session and felt no need to reschedule for now. The therapist and Nadia mutually agreed that Nadia could return whenever she wished. Three years later, Nadia made another appointment. When the therapist saw Nadia's name on his schedule and reviewed the notes from the earlier session, he was aware of his own curiosity about whether the earlier conversation had been helpful to Nadia. He welcomed her and began by asking what was better or different. Nadia described multiple positive changes in her life, including in her relationship with her mother. Now she wanted a consult on ways of dealing with her young adult daughter. At the end of the session she said, "It really helped to talk to you a few years ago, and it helped again today. Thank you."

In this case, the therapist discovered, 3 years later, that a previous visit was helpful. But there are also clients who do not reschedule (with their last therapist or any therapist at all) because they were *not* satisfied with something about the treatment. Without monitoring or feedback, the reasons for not returning are simply not known. To demonstrate efficacy, highly effective solution-focused and strategic therapists, like therapists of other orientations, may need to do more monitoring and obtain more feedback than they have done in the past.

"WHAT'S BETTER OR DIFFERENT?"

Follow-up sessions in solution-focused and strategic solution focused therapy frequently begin with this question. The response obtained provides a rich source of data about progress toward the goal. As Trepper et al. (2010) pointed out, clients often report noticeable improvements. In addition to using solution-focused methods to highlight and amplify these changes, solution-focused and strategic solution focused therapists can use this information to document progress toward the goal. Of course, some clients will report that things have remained the same or have gotten worse. This, too, can be documented. Clinically, this is typically followed by exploration of how the client has coped and/or what needs to happen to get back on track. Strategies may include using resources that are already in the client's life, along with collaborative discussion of what needs to happen today for this appointment to help in just the way the client wishes. In other words, the therapist is returning to the core principles of the model. If something done last time is not working, it may be time for the therapist, as well as the client, to do something different.

What are some possible ways of doing something different? The therapist might return to problem clarification, using collaborative conversation to be sure that the focus is on the highest priority area for change. It may be useful to reassess readiness for change. Maybe someone who appeared to be a customer is actually a complainant, or readiness may have shifted. Maybe it is time to look at the larger system, perhaps by inviting another member of the family to a session. Or the therapist and client could brainstorm the most unpredictable way that the client (or the therapist!) could react in this situation. The strategic therapist might think in terms of what might be the "180-degree opposite" of what was suggested before. Another approach normalizes changing slowly, slipping and getting back on track, and the combination of wanting to change and sometimes not wanting to change (what the author calls a "mini lesson on ambivalence"). This might lead to an experiment or homework idea like this: "Plan to go to the gym—and also expect to skip an occasional day exercising. Then get back on track next day, while remembering that we talked about 'maybe not wanting to.'"

If homework or an experiment of some kind was suggested, part of the monitoring may include checking out what happened with it. What the client did with the task (which may include ignoring it completely or transforming it in some way) is useful information. But failure to complete a solution-focused or strategic homework task does not necessarily mean that therapy is going poorly or that the suggestion was not useful. If the client did not do a task, the therapist will generally assume that something got in the way or that the task did not seem relevant or useful. The client may have changed the task into something more useful or discovered something better. Or the idea may have become a metaphor and produced change in a different way. If homework was not done, the strategic or solution-focused therapist generally will *not* suggest the same task in the same way. In the spirit of doing what works and changing what does not, the client has again communicated to the therapist that this client–therapist dyad needs to do something different.

However, sometimes insufficient follow-up on what was discussed last time interferes with progress. This was the case with Wendy, a client discussed in Chapter 4. Wendy began her session by saying

> I've been thinking about what I want from coming here. We talk a lot about what it would look like if I could make my changes. And that's helpful up to a point. But it's not enough. I can envision what I want, but I can't do it. If I could do it, I wouldn't be here. What I want to find out is what's stopping me.

Wendy knew what she wanted: completion of her home studio (for jewelry making), construction of a website for her jewelry business, a part-time job with seniors or children, a 10-pound weight loss, and more quality time with her children and husband. She said there were moments of great joy with her children and husband, but on other occasions, she was frustrated and felt like something was missing.

The therapist and Wendy reviewed the notes of her past sessions (10 past visits over 6 months), searching for clues about the obstacles—and about what they had been doing that was not working well enough. Review of those notes revealed that Wendy had many family responsibilities, which consumed much more time than she realized. In sessions she typically envisioned a goal and left with plans to implement some details of it. What neither the therapist nor Wendy had sufficiently incorporated into the solution scenarios was how the family tasks would get accomplished in the new scenario. At the next session, Wendy typically described something that was truly better but then set a new goal, claiming (and truly believing at the time) that this was the real priority. Then the same thing happened with the next goal. This clearly was not working.

What would be "something different"? The therapist and Wendy brainstormed this idea. Anticipating obstacles was one possibility, with careful discussion of how any ideas would need to allow time for the ever-present family responsibilities. Wendy said with a sigh, "Maybe I need to remember that I can't have it all." The therapist recalled aloud the words of a strategic therapist mentor: "If you move on to Problem Number Two before Problem Number One is fully resolved, Problem Number One will probably rear its ugly head again" (R. Fisch, personal communication, 1989, as cited in Quick, 2008, p. 26). Wendy said, "I remember something Bill Clinton is supposed to have said: 'Put everything in a box, pick one thing, and shut out everything else for a piece of time.'"

Wendy and the therapist reflected together: Was not focusing deeply on something for a sufficient chunk of time the "answer" to her question of "What stops me?" How long is "long enough" to focus, Wendy wondered. The therapist asked how Wendy made such decisions in other areas of her life. "For a crossword puzzle, when I've exhausted the possibilities, I put it down for a while," Wendy said. "Then after a while I pick it up again, and I do some more." After this important reevaluation of what was not working well enough, Wendy and the therapist decided the following: Choosing an area for focus; putting the other areas aside for now; finding her own pace; balancing the complementary, important parts of her life; and asking the therapist to remind her "not to start too many projects at once" all needed to become ingredients of Wendy's solution.

Wendy's situation brings to mind a comment from Fisch et al. (1982) about cases that were less successful. In these cases, the problem or the goal was unclear, and the therapist needed to return to problem clarification. One of the errors that the therapist and Wendy discovered was too much focus on solution elaboration without sufficient follow-up or problem clarification, at least until this session. McKergow (2010) commented that when solution-focused therapists think about the "tools" they use, they need to consider both "when to pick one up and when to put it down." With Wendy, it was time to "put down" the tool of solution elaboration (about projects), to "pick up" problem clarification, and then to return to solution elaboration at another level.

SCALING QUESTIONS

As described in previous chapters, scaling questions (and the inquiry that accompanies them) have multiple functions. They are a solution-focused intervention, one that invites most clients to recognize that they are already on the road to change, and they are also an assessment device. The most basic scaling question rates the client's perception of progress toward his or her own goal. In addition, scaling questions can be created to tap other variables, including perception of others' views of progress, readiness to take a next step, likelihood that one will do homework, and confidence that change can be maintained. Macdonald (2010) cited research indicating that scaling question responses appear to be as useful as scores on longer instruments in a number of domains.

When a scaling question number has been given at a first (or any previous) session, asking a client "Where are you now?" on that same scale provides a quantitative measure of progress. Obtaining scaling question responses at every session measures progress over time, and it provides an opportunity for adjusting the treatment in response to client needs. As with responses to the more open-ended "What's better or different?" inquiry described above, when the client's numbers are increasing, the therapist can elicit details about how the client made that happen, compliment the changes, and encourage building on them. If things are the same, the client can be invited to describe how past changes were sustained and how he or she kept things at the previous level. When there has been a decline, inquiry can focus on what the client needs to do to get back on track. With both unchanging and declining ratings, there is an opportunity to brainstorm together what the therapist and the client might be doing differently, as discussed above.

As Panayotov (2010) pointed out, not only can therapists trust clients to set their own goals; they can also trust clients to select the *process* that will be most helpful. Therefore, highly competent solution-focused and strategic therapists recognize that one of the best ways of adjusting treatment is to ask what the client thinks needs to happen. This may include a return to problem clarification, with questions such as these: "What do you think we need to be talking about?" and "What do you think is the most useful question I should be asking you right now?"

Some interesting research suggests that lower scaling question responses in solution-focused therapy may predict failure to return for a second session. Olsson and Wennerholm (2010) discovered a 50%

drop-out rate (between the first and second sessions) among clients who rated themselves below 3 on a scale where 10 was approaching "the miracle," compared to an 8% dropout rate for those who rated themselves at 3 or above. Based on some other data collected, the authors hypothesized that these clients experienced less solid therapeutic alliances. In a subsequent study, when scaling question responses were below 3, the therapists focused extra time and attention on the relationship. When this was done, the dropout rate at the second session declined to 10%.

FORMAL RATING TOOLS

Therapists of all orientations tend to assume that they can recognize when the therapeutic alliance is strong and when treatment is effective. However, it appears that therapists are not usually very good at predicting these things. Client ratings of both the therapeutic alliance and progress appear to be far better predictors of outcome than therapist ratings (Sperry, 2010b). In addition, the client's subjective perception of change early in treatment predicts positive outcome better than other measures (Orlinsky, Rønnestad, & Willutzki, 2003). These findings have clear implications: Therapists need to monitor their clients' views of the therapeutic alliance as well as outcome, and they need to be particularly vigilant about doing this right from the start of therapy.

In addition to the monitoring tools that are already embedded within solution-focused and strategic treatment, there are more formal methods, both paper-and-pencil and computer-based. Some therapists choose to use these on their own; others practice in settings that select a method to be used by all practitioners. Data can be compiled on individual therapists' effectiveness. This process can feel threatening to experienced therapists as well as to trainees, regardless of their orientation. In fact, it may feel *more* threatening to seasoned practitioners, who, unlike trainees, may not have had their work closely scrutinized for many years.

Duncan (2010) has emphasized that it is normal for therapists to feel some apprehension about being rated at every session. Actively soliciting feedback is scary! It can elicit fears and questions like these: What if I'm not very good? What if I'm average or, even worse, *below* average? How embarrassing that would be! In addition, low scores could affect my performance evaluation (for therapists working for an agency). Or if a list of therapists and their effectiveness is made public, potential future clients might choose another therapist! But, as Duncan (2010) pointed out, it is worth the risk, because feedback actually *improves* performance. It appears that therapists who receive formal feedback and adjust what they do in response to that feedback improve their performance, regardless of where they start out and regardless of orientation. In fact, therapists who receive *lower* initial ratings at earlier sessions and higher ones later get better results than those who get the highest ratings initially (Miller, 2008).

Two brief, user-friendly paper-and-pencil scales are widely used: the Session Rating Scale (SRS; Duncan et al., 2003) and the Outcome Rating Scale (ORS; Miller et al., 2003). The SRS, administered at the end of the session, measures how the session was for the client. It asks the client to mark, on a 10-centimeter scale, responses to the following four items: relationship (*I did not feel heard, understood, and respected* [one endpoint] versus *I did feel heard, understood, and respected* [other endpoint]), goals and topics (*We did/did not work on or talk about what I wanted to work on and talk about*), approach or method (*The therapist's approach is/is not a good fit for me*), and overall (*There was something missing in the session today* versus *Today's session was right for me*).

The ORS, administered at the beginning of the session, asks how the client has been feeling over the past week in the following four areas: individually (personal well-being), interpersonally (family, close relationships), socially (work, school, friendships), and overall (general sense of well-being). As with the SRS, the client makes a mark on a 10-centimeter line to indicate a response.

Like scaling questions, the ORS can be completed in different ways. Duncan (2010) noted that "mandated" clients sometimes answer the questions in a way that indicates few complaints. After completing the form a first time, the client can be asked to complete it with the answers he or she believes the referring person would give. (This might be the client's probation officer, parent, or spouse.) Then the therapist can ask, "What do you need to do to have that person agree with your view?" Like so many other tools used by solution-focused and strategic therapists, the scale that monitors progress can also become an intervention.

It might be noted here that when there is a decline on the ORS, the therapist needs to assess whether this reflects true deterioration or just the ups and downs of daily life. This holds true for declines on scaling question ratings and other scales as well. As J. Weakland (personal communication, Summer, 1986) often said, "Life is one damn thing after another." Duncan pointed out that when declines reflect such day-to-day changes, that does not necessarily mean that the therapy is not helping. Again, this is something that the therapist needs to clarify.

As suggested by these comments, *how* the therapist introduces and uses these tools is as important as the ratings themselves—and sometimes of even greater importance. It is here that the solution-focused and strategic attitude of genuinely *wanting* collaborative feedback appears most clearly, particularly at the higher levels of competency. These are *not* measures to be administered by a clerk or research assistant, with the therapist "blind" to the results. Just the opposite is the case! The goal is for the client and therapist to discuss the responses together, actively using the feedback to determine and fine-tune the next steps. Miller (2008) suggested introducing the scales in a way that creates "a culture of feedback." The therapist might say something like this:

> I want to be sure you get what you need in here. If we're going to see change, we should see it sooner rather than later. So every time you come in, I'm going to ask you to fill out this short form, so that we can see how you're doing in some important areas of your life. And at the end of every session, I have another short form for you, sort of to "take the temperature" of how we're doing, you and I, because that makes a difference in the results we get.

The following example is adapted from Miller's (2008) description of a therapist whose clients made particularly large gains. This therapist expressed a strong desire to know how she could improve the way she related to her clients, making it clear that she actively wanted this and that comments would not hurt her feelings. One day a client made a slightly lower rating on one item, and the therapist inquired about it. Probably embarrassed, the client initially backed off from elaborating. The therapist insisted: "Please, please, this is helpful to me to know." The client went on: "Well, it's your facial expression. When you have that look on your face, it feels like you're mad at me." The therapist continued to inquire about the details of what she did with her face, asking the client to demonstrate the expression that conveyed disapproval. Later, the therapist showed this reaction to her husband, who told her, "Yes, you do that. I've always hated that expression." This is an example of an extreme desire to understand and change how one comes across to clients—and in this case, it was associated with exceptional results.

The following example illustrates how using and actively discussing the results of the ORS and SRS can make a difference. Nicki came to therapy to discuss relationships in general. She focused on friendships and relationships at work. Her ORS scores were improving, and she gave high ratings on the SRS at her first three sessions. At end of session 4, Nicki's ratings were still at the top of the scale for the items measuring relationship and approach, but for the first time they were lower—just a bit—on the "goals" and "overall" items. The therapist expressed interest and asked what they might talk about next time in order to make the session more helpful. Nicki began to cry. She sobbed, "I've never had sex. I feel like a freak. And it bothers me so much that I'm embarrassed to talk about it, even in here. But I guess I have to." In this case, the SRS helped a client to bring up a topic that surfaced neither from intake forms nor from problem clarification.

There are electronic tracking systems available as well. One commonly used system, Polaris-MH (Polaris Health Directions, 2010), is a computer-based assessment system with an intake version and an update version for follow-up sessions. The client completes it at a computer in the waiting room, and an interpretive report is immediately delivered to the therapist's computer. Polaris measures symptoms, functional impairment, and belief that treatment will help. Advanced statistical techniques project an expected treatment response, based on multiple factors, including symptom severity, treatment history, and strengths. In the intake report, this information appears on a graph predicting the expected rate of decline in symptoms over time. The update reports plot "actual" versus "expected" ratings on this graph—an evidence-based way of determining whether treatment is helping and a useful visual tool for the therapist and client to view together.

The following example illustrates how Polaris ratings led to the identification of an area for change that had not previously been identified. Harry used his sessions to talk about how he wanted to handle dilemmas with his wife and his subordinates at work. He had not expressed concern about depression, anxiety, anger management, or substance use. Around the time of his sixth session, Polaris was implemented in the therapist's workplace. In this system, the first time the client completes the form is identified as the intake, even if, as was the case here, it is really in the middle of a course of treatment. Harry's intake scores suggested mood swings and concerns that home or work life was being affected by substance use.

The therapist and Harry read the Polaris report together, and both acknowledged that it suggested things they had not talked about before.

Harry said that there were more times than he wanted to admit when he and his wife had three bottles of wine, and this did contribute to their arguing and conflict. Harry often felt that his wife cared more about her young adult daughter (from a previous relationship) than she did about him. The therapist invited Harry to imagine how discussions about the daughter might go differently with less wine (or none at all). At the next session, Harry proudly announced that he was finding "non-wine ways to relax"; in addition, his relationship with his wife was better. His Polaris scores showed a decrease in symptoms as well.

One Polaris item asks about suicidal ideation. The regular monitoring of this important concern at every session is useful, and it sometimes leads to identification of this issue in clients who have denied any concerns about this in the past. Maggie, age 72, requested treatment for her "OCD [obsessive compulsive disorder] hoarding." She was making progress with the clutter in her house, and she often told her therapist how much she liked a solution-focused approach. On one occasion, however, Maggie endorsed "yes" to the "suicide ideation" item on Polaris. The therapist immediately inquired about what had happened. Maggie had learned that there might be some changes to her Medicare benefit, and she might have to pay much more for her medications and healthcare visits. She was thinking that she might have to declare bankruptcy, a legacy that she did not want to leave to her son. It had occurred to her that she had enough pills to kill herself. Maggie said, "You know, I almost didn't tell the truth on that computer thing. I thought: I come here for my clutter. I don't come here for depression or anything like that. And you like to hear the pretty stuff. I can't tell you that."

The therapist told Maggie, "I'm *so* glad you did tell me." This became an opportunity to discuss how Maggie could absolutely talk about things other than her clutter and that being solution-focused most emphatically did *not* mean that one could not talk about pain and dark feelings. The therapist invited Maggie to create a list of reasons for living. There was also discussion of plans for appealing the Medicare decision, riding through thoughts of killing herself without acting on them, and reaching out for support. Maggie and the therapist also discussed how, if bankruptcy became a serious alternative, that is a far better legacy to leave to a son as a coping tool than suicide. The therapist continued to monitor Maggie's Polaris responses. Conversations were still solution-focused but with an important difference: the important clarification that "doing what works" includes clear ways of addressing feelings of hopelessness and despair.

ARE THERE REASONS NOT TO USE SOLUTION-FOCUSED AND STRATEGIC METHODS?

It is legitimate to ask: With what populations do the solution-focused and strategic approaches *not* work? Bannick (2007) suggested that because solution-focused methods are so dependent upon hearing and honoring the client's voice, they may not work in situations where, for some reason, it is impossible to have a dialogue. One might hypothesize that in such situations, the therapist might attempt to understand the client's desires and goals on the basis of client behavior or other available data. When it is not possible to have a dialogue with the client, strategic therapists generally believe that therapy can still be done, as long as the therapist can have a dialogue with whoever is the primary customer or complainant.

As discussed throughout this book, an expectancy of positive change is an important contributor to change in psychotherapy. The therapist's belief that an approach will work interacts with the approach itself, creating what Miller (2008) has called "the model delivered." That is, a therapist who truly believes in the efficacy of solution-focused and strategic therapy will "deliver" a different (and probably more effective) treatment than a therapist who, for example, believes that only cognitive therapy can be helpful. (One might ask why a cognitive therapist would be using a solution-focused or strategic approach—or vice versa. This can occur in research studies, where the same therapist may be asked to use different methods. It can also happen where the supervisor or agency requires that specific methods be used.)

Clearly, the client's belief that an approach will be helpful makes a tremendous difference. People who actively request solution-focused and strategic approaches often respond quite well to these methods. The opposite can hold true as well: People who strongly believe that a different method will be most helpful may respond less well. For example, some clients who have had many courses of psychoanalytically oriented therapy may feel that they only can be helped by an approach that focuses heavily on the past. However, when Fiebelkorn, Chesmore, Ranney, and Vollmer (2010) evaluated the effect of client preferences (for therapeutic

125

modality) on outcome, they discovered that collaborative discussion of what a modality offers and how it works resulted in a positive effect on outcome. This kind of collaborative discussion appeared to be more effective than simply letting the client choose the approach, and it was clearly more effective than having the therapist alone select and apply a method.

When working with a client who has experienced benefit from past therapy (of any orientation), solution-focused and strategic therapists can discover what was most helpful. They can look for ways in which the client can remember lessons learned and return to "what worked" in the past. Fiske (2008) has commented that the solution-focused therapist can be like a magpie, shamelessly keeping an eye open for "shiny objects." Just as the magpie weaves a scrap of tin foil into her nest (even though it is not a natural material, as a twig or leaf might be), solution-focused and strategic therapists weave any possible thread into an approach tailored to this client's needs. Then, as emphasized in this chapter, they monitor what works and what does not and adjust what they do in response.

9

Maintaining Treatment Gains and Planning for Termination

Continuing and building on "what works" is central in solution-focused and strategic therapy. This chapter addresses the core competency involving evaluation of progress and preparation for termination in the strategic and solution-focused therapies. It discusses length of treatment—single session, brief, or intermittent—and covers how therapists and clients collaboratively make decisions about frequency of sessions and when to discontinue therapy. Sometimes the plan includes a "maintenance dose of psychotherapy," scheduled booster sessions, or an invitation to return if needed. The plan is tailored to individual client needs and influenced by progress toward goals, healthcare system variables (including insurance coverage and availability of appointments), and client preferences. Solution-focused conversations about a future that include "slips and recovery" and several strategic tools add a "relapse prediction and management" component to the work. The "doing what works and changing what doesn't" perspective, openly shared with clients, is a tool to use for maintenance of gains long after treatment has ended. As therapists and clients plan for termination, they review together both progress toward goals and feelings (often mixed) about the process. An acceptance-based component (that some discomfort, challenges, and patterns may continue to be present) may be balanced by a change-focused perspective that celebrates changes made, plans for continued growth, and previous success in getting back on track after slips.

WHEN TO TERMINATE

As Weakland et al. (1974) and Quick (2008) have pointed out, brevity is not the *goal* of the strategic and solution-focused therapies, but it is often a *result* of using these approaches. The plan for termination begins during treatment planning, done collaboratively at the beginning of treatment and discussed throughout. Sometimes strategic and solution-focused therapists plan to work within a specified number of sessions. As noted previously, the Mental Research Institute (MRI) Brief Therapy Project team used an "up to 10 sessions" model. If the problem was resolved in fewer sessions, the remaining ones remained "in the bank." In other settings, strategic therapists often work without a specified number of appointments, maintaining maneuverability and tailoring the length of treatment (like all other components of treatment) to client needs.

Solution-focused therapy is typically brief. How brief is brief? As discussed in Chapter 6, de Shazer (as cited in D. Simon, 1993, p. 1) responded to that question with this response: "Not one session more than necessary." Solution-focused therapists and their clients discuss number and spacing of sessions as they go along. When scaling question numbers rise (but are not yet at a 10), solution-focused therapists may ask, "If you can stay at x, will that be good enough?" Often the answer is yes.

The first session of strategic solution focused therapy includes discussion of treatment details, one of which is the length of treatment. The number of sessions and intervals between sessions will be flexibly tailored to client needs, as well as taking into account practical considerations. There is not an automatic assumption that appointments will occur every week.

The therapist may point out that the plans may well change as therapy proceeds. Sometimes at the beginning of treatment, a client may want to come more often, with longer intervals between sessions desired later on. Some clients like the idea of "booster sessions," similar to "well-baby visits." Shorter intervals between sessions can also be planned when needed.

The therapist inquires about what the client wants and expects. The client may be viewing this appointment as a one-time consultation; he or she may not have been expecting to return at all. The author's experience is that most clients do *not* automatically request weekly appointments. The ones who *do* want to come weekly are often people who have been in weekly therapy before! When that is the request, and appointments are available, this of course can be done, with reevaluation along the way.

In integrated healthcare, solution-focused and strategic therapy consultations in the primary care setting, with feedback to other healthcare providers, are a variation of single session therapy.

As Quick (2008) pointed out, often strategic solution focused therapy is practiced in the spirit of a family practice/intermittent care model. Termination does not mean that all problems are resolved forever or that a return to therapy means that a prior course of treatment did not work. When the client encounters another "bump on the road of life" (whether in the same area or a different one), he or she can always return.

Some clients face longstanding medical, social, interpersonal, and behavioral issues that may be present over many years. Lipchik (2002) noted that therapy sometimes involves both grieving losses and building a future, and therapists help clients to discover and use both past and potential resources. Therapy is not necessarily long term, but sometimes it does continue longer than is typically the case. Some clients who have in the past received diagnoses of "serious psychiatric illness" thrive with a "maintenance dose" of solution-focused therapy (J. Simon & Nelson, 2007).

The results of a small study indicate how hard it is to predict when clients will end therapy, even in the presence of a plan for a specific number of sessions. In this project, clients were referred to the same therapist for strategic solution focused therapy that was specifically described as brief therapy, of six to eight sessions. Of the 99 clients seen over a 3-year period, 34% actually came six to eight times. Thirty percent came once or twice, 29% attended three to five sessions, and 5% had many more appointments. (The insurance coverage did allow for additional appointments.) Analyses of the scores on outcome measures indicated a decrease in symptoms for all groups. It is possible that more sophisticated analyses would have revealed more subtle differences among clients who attended different numbers of sessions. But from the available data, what is most striking is that even when a project attempted to define a specific number of sessions, clients selected a number that fit for them. In this case, the number selected was different from what the project had planned 66% of the time (Quick, 2007).

Some therapy—perhaps more than many therapists want to acknowledge—stops because of external factors. Therapist trainees complete their placements at agencies and rotations, healthcare insurance coverage and policies change, and clients move, and these changes are not timed to coincide with clinical needs. In theory, treatment can continue with new therapists and in new settings; in practice, it often does not. Therapists therefore need to be prepared to address termination with clients when it happens for reasons other than clinical ones. Therapists at higher levels of competence are better able to make termination a positive experience even when its timing is less than ideal.

The following example illustrates how strategic solution focused therapists at different levels of competence might handle an unexpected termination. Caitlin, age 23, entered treatment because of distress about her relationship with her boyfriend, Jeremy. She had been having an affair with a coworker; Jeremy discovered it from pictures on her cell phone and asked Caitlin to move out. Caitlin did not want to lose Jeremy. During the five sessions that she was seen, Caitlin made some significant changes, including stopping drinking, going to Alcoholics Anonymous meetings, discontinuing her affair, and trying to communicate more openly with Jeremy. At session 6, Caitlin announced that this would be her last visit. She had been "fired" and would lose the insurance coverage that allowed her to see her therapist.

Therapist A, who was at the beginning level of competency, reacted internally to Caitlin's news with disappointment, frustration, and some anger. Therapist A had been hoping to present Caitlin in a seminar on solution-focused therapy, but now Caitlin was going to be a "dropout." There would not be an opportunity to see Caitlin create her "miracle" (rebuilding the relationship with Jeremy), taper sessions, and plan a termination. Therapist A had not yet learned—or did not remember—that termination in the solution-focused and strategic therapies can invite building on client strengths even when it occurs unexpectedly. Deciding not to bother with trying to be solution-focused for the remainder of the session, Therapist A said, "Oh, that's a shame you have to stop. Hmm. I think the agency needs you to fill out some form if it's your last time here" and spent the rest of the time on paperwork.

Therapist B, who was at the "adequate competency" stage, had the same initial reaction. But Therapist B went on to ask, "So, how can you make this change a good thing for you?" Caitlin replied that she already had a new job, with new insurance. She had seen the downsizing coming and realized that it presented an opportunity to get away from seeing her former lover every day. The therapist complimented Caitlin on her careful thinking and planning and encouraged her to continue the good things she had begun.

Therapist C, who was at a higher level of competence, responded as Therapist B did. In addition, Therapist C asked whether Caitlin wanted to review the changes made since her first visit. Caitlin did, and they reviewed her progress together. "How will you keep your good changes going, even when it's tough?" Therapist C asked. Caitlin replied that she planned to seek therapy through her new insurance.

Therapist C: So, if you decide to sign a release for me to talk to your new therapist, and that therapist calls me up and asks me what helps you most when things are hard, what should I say?

Caitlin: [mumbling, twisting a lock of hair] I don't know.

Therapist C: [smiling] How do you think I would answer that question?

Caitlin: Probably that I *do* know what's good for me.

Therapist C: What else?

Caitlin: And I eventually do it. Maybe not in the most elegant way, but I do it.

Therapist C: Wow. Can I add one more thought? [Caitlin nods] May I tell your new therapist that even if your first answer to a question is "I don't know," to keep asking? Because you really *do* know.

Caitlin: [with a wry smile] Sure, you can tell them that. And I guess I need to remember it, too. And maybe I'll tell Jeremy that, too.

EVALUATION OF OUTCOME

As discussed in the previous chapter, ongoing monitoring of progress should occur throughout treatment. Consequently, evaluation of outcome at the completion of therapy is not a distinct phenomenon; rather, it is a continuation of what ideally has been occurring all along. And because, as described above, therapy often ends sooner than predicted, this means that data are available for the "last" session, whether or not it was a planned termination. When measures like the Session Rating Scale (SRS; Duncan et al., 2003), the Outcome Rating Scale (ORS; Miller et al., 2003), and Polaris-MH (Polaris Health Directions, 2010) are used, the ratings at the final session are important data points. When scaling question responses are recorded, these too can provide pre- and posttreatment measures. Other measures, such as the *Beck Depression Inventory II* (Beck, 1996) and the Solution Building Inventory (Smock, 2011) also can be administered both before and after treatment. Any of these instruments can also be administered at follow-up, when the setting permits this, for measurement of maintenance of gains over time.

131

The Doing What Works Group, an up to five session solution-focused group, collects scaling question data and members' narrative comments each week. Every session of this group ends with members sharing their responses to the "What do you most want to remember?" question, with a "tradition" of "graduating" (terminating) members speaking first. The forms are both a clinical tool and a source of outcome data for research, and the data have documented positive movement toward client-generated goals (Quick, 2008; Quick & Gizzo, 2007).

HOW TO TERMINATE

In brief strategic therapy, Fisch et al. (1982) noted that termination generally occurs without celebration or fanfare. It is not particularly regarded as a special event. As described previously, MRI Brief Therapy Project clients who finished the work in fewer than ten sessions were encouraged to "leave the remaining sessions in the bank." Fisch and Schlanger (1999) pointed out that clients do not need to "go the whole distance." Simply getting started on the road to change is often sufficient. There is an assumption that once a person discontinues an unsuccessful attempted solution, positive changes will continue to steer that person away from returning to what did not work. There is often a "restraint from change" message that cautions that one should "go slow"[1] on too much additional change too soon.

In solution-focused therapy, as in strategic therapy, termination occurs when the goal is reached, when the problem is resolved, or when things are working "well enough." Lipchik (2002) stated that the ideal termination occurs when the client describes a solution, the therapist and client agree to meet after a longer interval of time, and the solution is still working. The termination process may include a review of where the client was at intake, solution scenarios envisioned, and pieces of those solutions that are now happening. The author often uses the clinical record as a tool in this review for client and therapist to read together. There can be discussion—and celebration—of what worked and inquiry about "How did you do that?!" If the "What do you want to remember?" question was asked at the end of sessions, those answers are useful to review as well. In strategic solution focused therapy, there may also be reflection together about realizations about what does *not* work well enough, especially when the "doing what works" philosophy

132

has been openly discussed. This can lead to planning ways of maintaining change and preparing for future challenges, described in the following section.

RELAPSE PREDICTION, PREVENTION, AND MANAGEMENT

Relapse prevention planning was originally discussed in detail in the substance abuse treatment literature (Marlatt & Gordon, 1985). Sperry (2010a) noted that teaching clients to become their own therapists can sometimes be considered to be the ultimate goal of therapy. Brief strategic therapy addresses this issue by avoiding what Fisch et al. (1982) called a "cheering send-off" that overtly states (or covertly implies) that everything will be fine from now on. Instead, the strategic therapist may recommend refraining from active attempts to create additional change for a while. There may be a suggestion to expect or even deliberately create some exacerbation of the problem. This will provide an opportunity for the client to practice new skills. The therapist might use an analogy like this: "You don't really know that the roof is fixed until it rains. And since (in southern California!) that may not happen for a few months, maybe you should squirt the hose onto the roof, just to see what happens."

Solution-focused and strategic solution focused therapy often include more highlighting of client gains than is typical in strategic therapy. However, here too, there is no implication that challenges will not arise in the future. The therapist may remind the client about envisioned futures that include slips and recovery and use the strategic tools that add a relapse prediction and management component to the work. There will be inquiry about what feels right to the client as a next step, about possible setbacks that will arise, and how the client will recognize these and get back on track.

CASE EXAMPLE: JACK

The following case example illustrates a discussion of termination. Jack, a 47-year-old computer scientist, is married and has two young children. This is his seventh session. Jack was first seen 3 months earlier, following

133

stressful interactions with his boss and a poor performance evaluation at work—the first critical review he had ever received. Jack had felt anxious and angry. He consulted his primary care physician, who prescribed an antidepressant and referred Jack for therapy. Jack met the criteria for major depression, single episode, mild, generalized anxiety disorder (probably longstanding), and occupational problem. He attended four sessions at 2-week intervals, reporting positive changes and requesting longer intervals between subsequent appointments. Session 6, one month earlier, had ended with the therapist's suggestion to continue what was working, to expect moments of distress, and to notice how he got back on track.

Therapist: Hey, Jack, welcome back. Did you do our little form on the [waiting room] computer today?

Jack: Sure did.

Therapist: Let's take a look at it. [Together they view the Polaris-MH update report on the computer screen.] Look at that: Your scores are still low. [Low scores reflect few symptoms on this system.]

Jack: Yeah, doing good.

Therapist: Tell me about it. What's better or different since last time?

Jack: Yeah, I'm good, really good. My boss was away for two weeks. That sure helped! But even since he's back, I'm okay.

Therapist: Cool. How are you doing that, staying okay?

Jack: Well, a couple things, I think. I'm laying low, letting the beam of light shine on someone else for a while. Let someone else take the flak. And part of it is, we're making great progress on the design project. Great project meeting last week. And I'm also sending out some resumes, quietly, just to see what else is out there. No nibbles yet, but I'm looking. And Ann [Jack's wife] and I are talking about it, about how I might want to change jobs or even take a break from work for a while. And it really seems like she's okay with it. It really does. At first when she said that I didn't really think she meant it, but now I do.

Therapist: What lets you know this is real for her?

Jack: Little things. Like when we were talking about putting low-water landscaping in the back and she said "Maybe we can do that when you're on your sabbatical."

Therapist: Your sabbatical.

Jack: Yeah, neat word, huh?

Therapist: Yeah. I like that word. Hey, Jack, I'm curious if you had an opportunity to have what we called an "anger flash," so you could practice getting back on track?

Jack: Sort of. When old Mr. Know-It-All came back from his leave and I tried to treat him like a normal person and ask him about his trip, he just sort of ignored me. I thought, "You jerk, you have no social skills at all. No wonder no one likes you. No wonder *I* don't like you. No wonder I'd have been just as happy if your plane had crashed." Which is a pretty horrible thought. But I didn't freak out or anything.

Therapist: Wow, how did you manage not to freak at that thought?

Jack: I don't know, maybe just thinking, "The guy *is* socially retarded." And it makes sense that I hate him. That's just where my mind goes. And almost being able to laugh at myself. Like that saying—wasn't it Ronald Reagan who said this?—"There you go again."

Therapist: Wow, that's huge.

Jack: Yeah, it is. I mean, it never got to where it was when I first came here, that flash of worrying that I might really do something to him. But even if I did have that flash, I know I wouldn't *really* do anything to hurt him. I'd just let him dig his own hole and fall in it, because if he keeps acting like he does with his employees, it's just a matter of time till someone else lets higher administration know. He'll get his. But it's not going to be me who does the job. He really must be an unhappy person to treat people the way he does, and I'm going to do what I need to do to take care of myself. And if that means changing jobs or taking a break from working at all for a while, so be it. Ann's okay with it. Our kids can still go to college. It's not a deal breaker in my life.

Therapist: Really. So, Jack, if things stay the way they are now, and you stay the way you are, will that be good enough?

Jack: I think it will. Yeah, I remember we talked last time about how I'll know when I'm ready to do this on my own. Maybe I'm ready now.

Therapist: Like ready to not schedule a follow-up appointment?

Jack: Yeah. What do you think? You know how you always ask me what I want to talk about?

Therapist: Yup, I'm so predictable. [Both laugh]

Jack: I think today I want to talk about how I'll know that I'm ready to stop coming. If I can trust my sense of it.

Therapist: I'm thinking about how you came to know that having the flash "What if I hurt him?" doesn't mean you're *really* going to hurt him. How did you do that?

Jack: Just accepting the flash. And him, in a way, that he's an asshole, and that I hate him. And that I have choices.

Therapist: And I'm thinking about how you came to trust that Ann is really okay with it if you take a sabbatical.

Jack: Passage of time. Her saying it not just once. Talking about it together.

Therapist: Awesome. What else?

Jack: Maybe the sense that it'll be okay. That I'll be okay. And maybe that taps into my faith. That I don't have to have everything planned out for the rest of my life. That I don't have to stay in this job forever to be a good husband and a good father. No matter what my father-in-law and I talked about years ago.

Therapist: There are so many ways to be an amazing husband and father.

Jack: Really.

Therapist: Jack, sometimes it's useful in a last appointment to recap our conversations together. Would it be useful to take a few minutes to do that?

Jack: Yeah, that would be cool. I'd like that.

Together Jack and the therapist reviewed their time together. Jack remembered panicking when he had the sudden thought "What if I hurt my boss?" after receiving a less than stellar review from a boss who had been increasingly critical and condescending. Jack had felt a strong urge to impulsively quit his job. At the same time, he could not stop thinking about a conversation he had had years ago with his now-deceased father-in-law: "I'll always take care of your daughter. She'll be the nurse who married the computer scientist." Jack felt that he could not leave his job. He saw no options and felt trapped and panicky.

Jack's complaint had been the intrusive aggressive thoughts, and his goal was to "not have them." What would let him know that he was moving in the right direction? Talking to his wife about something other than his boss, he said. What had Jack tried, in his best attempts to "not have the thoughts"? "Don't think about it." This was not working. The therapist and Jack had talked about the opposite of this: *expecting* the thoughts to be there, in view of everything that was going on, and riding through them.

Jack and the therapist remembered together the "worst" thing that could have been recommended: "You have to go to a psychiatric hospital." The "best" had been: "We can do something about it." Jack also remembered that the therapist had told him about the availability of some brief time off work, if he ever needed it. Here is what Jack had wanted to remember from that first session: "I don't have to go to a hospital. I have options. Instead of bringing home bad things from work, I can bring home some off-the-wall story."

Review of the notes from subsequent sessions revealed that Jack had realized almost immediately that he did not have to stay in this job forever in order to fulfill his promise to Ann's dad. Jack felt freer to explore other job possibilities. Although he was not immediately finding anything that seemed like a serious option, "just looking" made a positive difference. Jack remembered this question the therapist had asked: "Will I be more helpful if I give you a gentle nudge to get out there and look or a message to take all the time you need?" (The answer had been "Both.") Jack also remembered seriously considering the possibility of requesting some time off work—and then deciding against it.

There had also been an unexpected positive development: the reemergence of a work project that had been on hold for many months. This gave Jack something else to focus on at work and to discuss at home. (This is an example of how factors outside psychotherapy can make powerful contributions to positive change.) Jack had some true expertise in the area of this project. He had several opportunities to make useful recommendations to his team (including the boss), and these boosted his confidence in his ability to eventually find a more satisfying job. Jack remembered the therapist's encouragement to "go slow" and to consider what he would "hate most" in a new job or supervisor. "That was so different from what everyone else was telling me," Jack said.

As Jack looked at more options—including staying at his current job and letting his boss "dig his own hole and fall in it"—he talked about these things at home. He was surprised to hear Ann's support for the idea of his changing jobs. He used one session to puzzle aloud: What might account for her changed attitude? She used to be so cautious, like her dad. Was it because their house was now paid off? Was she looking at her own job differently? Was this a shifting of her priorities at midlife? Jack clearly remembered the therapist's suggestion when he had wondered about this: "You said to me— and I remember just how you looked out the window, and then back at me— you asked me, 'How do you think Ann would answer that question?' And I went—'Duh! Dude, you *could* just ask her.'" Jack did so, and he discovered

137

that all of his ideas were actually accurate. Talking together, about their hopes and fears and plans for the future, drew Ann and Jack closer.

Therapist: So, as we talk about all these changes you've made, what stands out most to you?

Jack: That I have options. You said that my first time here, I think. And that Ann's with me. And that my boss really is an asshole—at least that it's okay to think that. And that I probably *will* quit this job some day. I'm not leaving today or tomorrow, but I don't have to stay there forever. And that as long as I'm there, my quirky little mind will probably go bizarre places when Mr. Social Retard is at his finest. And that I can almost laugh at it. That's a long answer, but there's a bunch of things.

Therapist: Yes. There really are. You know, Jack, as I reflect on our time together, and all the things you've changed and realized, I'm struck by how huge all these things are. And I'm thinking about how you started our journey wanting to get rid of the thoughts toward your boss, and how on one level, you have, and at another level, you've also done so much more. And part of that is realizing how your mind does its thing, and being able to go "There you go again."

Jack: Yeah. I like how you put that.

Therapist: We need to wind down in a few minutes, and if I'm hearing you right, this will be an end for us for now. [Jack nods.] And as we end, I'm thinking about that philosophy I told you about: If it works, do it. If it doesn't work, don't do it. Do something different. So, what can I say, Jack? I invite you to keep doing what works, and when your boss does his thing, and your mind does its thing, to notice how you keep getting through it. And you know where I am if you need me.

Jack: Thank you. This all was pretty awesome.

Therapist: You're welcome. You're very welcome.

MIXED FEELINGS ABOUT TERMINATION: STRATEGIC AND SOLUTION-FOCUSED PERSPECTIVES

Fisch et al. (1982) directly discussed the fact that clients sometimes want to continue therapy after a complaint has been resolved or beyond the

10-session limit used in the Brief Therapy Project. Other clients want to stop therapy sooner. These authors stated that when one problem has been resolved and the client wants to work on another, the therapist should use the strategy of going slow, which may include taking some time before scheduling a session to address another problem. In the opposite situation, when the client wants to terminate before the therapist sees problem resolution, Fisch et al. commented that the therapist should resist any temptation to urge the client to remain. This statement implies that therapists may well experience such an urge. However, even in the presence of such feelings, these authors recommend that the therapist take a one-down position, which may include acknowledging that he or she has not helped enough. Asking for feedback is also part of the recommended strategy: "What, in your best judgment, do you feel was done or not done that may have hindered your resolving your problem?" (Fisch et al., p. 184).

Solution-focused and strategic solution focused therapists also recognize that both clients and therapists may have mixed feelings about termination. Although guided by theory that says that therapy should not continue any longer than needed for creation of the desired change, Lipchik (2002) pointed out that therapists can become attached to clients for reasons of their own. And because, to paraphrase Beyebach (2007), "Solution-focused therapists are just so nice," clients may be reluctant to terminate a relationship that celebrates their strengths and uniqueness. The therapeutic relationship may be very different from other relationships in clients' lives.

In strategic solution focused therapy, the conversation about termination, like other conversations throughout the treatment, can include discussion about the normalcy of mixed feelings about the process. The client—and, when this is the case, the therapist—can acknowledge that they have felt a connection during their visits together and that there may be some reluctance about bringing the process to an end. Building on the Ericksonian tradition that is part of solution-focused and strategic therapy, the therapist may invite the client to "carry my voice with you," if this feels helpful. Part of relapse management can involve inviting the client to imagine a conversation with the therapist about a future challenge. In the spirit of slightly making fun of his or her own predictability, the therapist might say, "When you think it might be helpful to have a conversation with me, you might think, with a little chuckle: 'S(he) was so predictable! What was that question s(he) used to ask me? And what else did s(he) used to say?'" Rather than viewing this as "unhealthy dependency" or something to be avoided, the therapist can actively encourage continuing what was useful. An acceptance-based component (that challenges may recur) again can be balanced by a change-focused perspective that utilizes memories of the therapy, and of the therapist, for getting back on track after slips.

NOTE

1. Although it may be more correct grammatically to say "go slowly," "go slow" was the language often used by the MRI therapists and that usage has become part of the strategic therapy tradition.

10

Practicing the Solution-Focused and Strategic Therapies With Cultural and Ethical Sensitivity

This chapter discusses how solution-focused and strategic therapists address the following two competencies: first, planning and implementing tailored and culturally sensitive interventions and, second, making ethically sensitive decisions. The therapist deliberately discovers, respects, and utilizes client variables in tailoring treatment to client needs, language, social resources, and preferences. The "one size does *not* fit all" perspective can decrease well-intended but often erroneous assumptions that clients from similar ethnic, racial, or religious backgrounds will have the same symptoms and preferences. Case examples illustrate the process.

Like therapists of any orientation, solution-focused and strategic therapists need to know and adhere to the ethical principles of their professions. Maintaining confidentiality, avoiding conflicts of interest, and other ethical issues are addressed in this chapter from the perspective of doing what works to respect the client's values, dignity, and rights. It is emphasized that "doing what works" emphatically does *not* mean that "any means justify the end." Just the opposite is true. When there is a paradoxical component to some strategic interventions (which sometimes predict the presence or recurrence of symptoms or patterns the client wishes to eliminate), the strategic solution focused therapist is transparent about the phenomenon. Therapists and clients discuss together the existential reality that symptoms and patterns do reappear and that anticipating and coping with them are often critical ingredients of the solution.

CULTURAL CONSIDERATIONS

Kluckhohn (1951) defined *culture* as an acquired and transmitted pattern of shared meaning, feeling, and behavior that characterizes a distinctive group. However, more recent definitions refer to a more complex phenomenon. Culture includes demographic characteristics (such as place of residence), status (educational and economic levels), ethnographic variables (nationality, ethnicity), language, and affiliations. People who differ from each other on any of these dimensions can "experience the world in different ways, whether those differences are based on internal difference, external difference in the way they are treated by others, or a combination of the two" (Connerly & Pederson, 2005, p. 4).

Sperry (2010a) described a number of variables that the culturally competent therapist needs to consider. These include cultural identity, degree of acculturation, and cultural views of what causes illness and what cures it. It is also relevant to know whether clients feel that they have experienced discrimination because of culture, religion, disability, sexual identity, or other factors. Dobbins (2010) pointed out that some identities are "invisible." He also noted that cultural competence is a requirement for evidence-based treatment even when the therapist and client are of the same race and gender. Therapists at lower levels of competence may err by failing to assess these dimensions. Fields (2010) pointed out that another type of error involves *overestimating* the impact of culture in a particular case. An example of this is a therapist assuming that a Chinese client would not want to express feelings and then discovering that the client enjoyed talking about her culture—and expressing feelings in stories she told.

Psychotherapy can be culturally competent in multiple ways, and Sperry (2010b) described the following three possibilities. First, there are cultural interventions, which use healing methods from the client's culture or invite collaboration with healers such as *curanderos* or sheiks. Second, culturally sensitive therapy, which directly addresses cultural beliefs and customs, may be helpful with clients at lower levels of acculturation. Third, there are culturally sensitive interventions, which are conventional interventions that have been adapted to a client's cultural characteristics.

The author has heard feedback on required "cultural diversity training" from multiple predoctoral psychology interns. A consistent theme has emerged. The training seen as *less* helpful comes across in this way: "Latinos do this; Asians do that; do (or don't do) this with African American men, or with gay couples …" Trainees (some of whom identified with the groups being discussed) often perceived this input as stereotyping. The trainings experienced as *more* helpful were those that encouraged trainees to consider the many facets of their own identities and the assumptions that they bring to the session. With increased awareness of their own reactions, they reported that they were better able to listen to what the client brings.

In a discussion of cultural competence, Lopez (2009) used the metaphor of baseball. He noted that expert pitchers have very different styles: Some throw with their arms close to the body; others hold their arms far out to the side. He commented that some coaches try to make everyone pitch the same way, and that something that was supposed to help (coaching) may result in a pitcher being trained to do something that is less effective. He said, "The Cubans have the right idea [regarding baseball coaching]. If a guy does something and it works for him, they don't train him out of it." This perspective is highly consistent with solution-focused and strategic techniques and attitudes. For clients and for therapists, one size definitely does not fit all.

SOLUTION-FOCUSED AND STRATEGIC PERSPECTIVES ON CULTURAL COMPETENCE

Tailoring treatment to these variables has always been a central component of all strategic and solution-focused practice. The MRI brief strategic therapy team emphasized the importance of assessing "position" variables, which include cultural perceptions of why people behave as they do and what accounts for change. For example, the therapist assesses whether children are thought to misbehave because they are "bad" or "sad" in the client's culture—and in the client's family in particular.

Solution-focused therapists also emphasize careful attention to detail. de Shazer and Berg discussed this in an interview with Short (1997). Berg commented that:

> ... [I]t is a big deal now to study generalities about ethnic families, about Asian families, Hispanic families, African American families, etc., but I think that is ignoring the details. Even among the Asian families there are so many varieties. With ethnic families I think there is even a greater need to pay attention to the individual family details. (p. 19)

de Shazer added that if the client wants to talk about the problem, the therapist needs to allow that to happen—and to notice the details there—because those will provide the material needed to build a solution.

When solution-focused and strategic therapists hear stories of loss and relocation following war and immigration from a beloved native land, they listen for strengths that suggest resilience. A Vietnamese woman's goal was "to be strong and hang in there" with her difficult husband until her children were older. She had come to the United States at age 11; she had lived in a refugee camp and learned English. She did far more than survive: She thrived in a new culture, going on to college and establishing strong friendships. Her strength and ability to thrive in the face of adversity became ingredients of solution in her current situation.

When miracle question inquiry is done, the therapist needs to assure that it is conducted in a manner consistent with the client's views. The reader may remember that the original miracle question grew from a client's language (and possibly her cultural and religious beliefs as well): "It would take a miracle to solve my problem." As noted throughout this book, miracle questions are quite effective with many people who are not particularly religious. But when a client is vocally and adamantly "anti-religion," that might indicate that *any* reference whatsoever to miracles would not be a good idea. If the client is raging about "the religious kooks all over our community—they talk about miracles and crap like that," the therapist who is listening with respect definitely does *not* respond with an invitation to imagine that a miracle has happened! Here, a culturally sensitive invitation to imagine a preferred future will use different language (for example, "Imagine that our conversation today has helped you in just the way you hoped").

Some solution-focused therapists at a lower level of competency might not consider cultural variables, and they might use the same kind of miracle question inquiry for every client. Others might recognize that the standard miracle question would not be appropriate but not know how to create alternate strategies for eliciting views of a preferred future. At higher levels of competency, therapists will create variations on the miracle question or use other kinds of future-focused inquiry and solution-focused tools, tailoring the details in a way that is congruent with the client's world.

In family sessions of solution-focused and strategic solution focused therapy, typically the therapist asks the miracle question of each family member, including children. That procedure might seem disrespectful to some families. In American Samoa, for example, children are expected not to speak in the presence of elders (Clay, 2010). In some cultures, women may not be expected to express independent opinions in the presence of men. The therapist who listens for and respects these norms—and who wants to ask a miracle question in a way that will be appropriate for the family—therefore may want to adapt the inquiry. Explaining the procedure to the person with highest status in the family may result in that member requesting that the other family members respond to the therapist's questions. In some families, the therapist may choose to meet with family members separately.

Respecting the norms of different generations also becomes a component of therapy. One therapist told a story of an adolescent who avoided eye contact with the therapist. Head down and thumbs moving, the girl seemed far more interested in texting on her phone than in anything going on in the room. The therapist was thinking about how to bring this up when she noticed that her own phone kept vibrating. It was extremely unusual for anyone to text her so frequently. Although she did not usually do so during sessions, she glanced at her phone— and discovered that the young client in her office was texting her, using a medium that felt safer than words. The therapist texted back, and therapy continued.

CASE EXAMPLES: CULTURAL FACTORS AS INGREDIENTS OF THE SOLUTION

The first case is adapted from a story told by Fiske (2009) about a young First Nations man from northern Canada. Because of a disability, this young man was unable to hunt. He was despondent. For most men his age, in his culture, hunting is the reason for living. The young man sat with his grandfather around the fire. His grandfather said, "Your despair is like a wolf. It will eat your soul. But hope is also a wolf." Grandfather paused. After a long silence, the young man asked, "Which wolf will win in this fight?" Grandfather replied, "The wolf that you feed." This is an example of what Sperry calls a cultural intervention, as described above. A non–First Nation therapist might tell this story to a client to convey a message to "feed your hope rather than your despair."

The following case, adapted from a client described by Fields (2010), illustrates how understanding of the client's culture, his view of the problem, and the details of his life contributed to the solution. Ben-Ya-Meen, age 54, came to the United States from Bosnia with his daughter to escape the war. He had lost his wife, his friends, and his work. Ben-Ya-Meen had been waking suddenly with nightmares, feeling that something was terribly wrong. Ben-Ya-Meen spoke little English, and therapy needed to be conducted through a translator. The therapist was never sure of the accuracy of the translation (in either direction). There seemed to be little evidence of a strong therapeutic alliance, and Ben-Ya-Meen seemed frustrated by the therapist's attempts to explain posttraumatic stress disorder.

The therapist asked Ben-Ya-Meen about his life, and he learned that Ben-Ya-Meen enjoyed chess and was actually quite good at it. The interpreter then joined the conversation. He knew of a small group of Bosnian immigrants, and some of them also played chess. Ben-Ya-Meen began to meet with them at a local coffee shop, and he found someone to play chess with. That man had also lost several family members in the war.

Fields (2010) wrote, "Never did [the client] talk in detail about his trauma, work on relaxation techniques, identify triggers, or take medication" (p. 199). What made a difference was social support and building on his strengths. The author noted that "addressing the cultural dynamics became more important than initiating a treatment plan" (p. 199). A solution-focused or strategic therapist would say: What this therapist did *was* the treatment plan, at least from a strategic solution focused perspective.

Abu Raiya and Pargament (2010) discussed conducting religiously integrated psychotherapy with Muslim clients. Although they did not specifically describe their approach as solution-focused, they too described an approach fully consistent with discovering and amplifying what is supportive and helpful in the client's world. The following case is adapted from a client described by these authors. Farooq, age 20, is a young American Muslim of Middle Eastern descent. He has not been attending his college classes. Farooq has recently experienced multiple losses, including his father's incurable illness, the loss of a relationship, and a sports injury that resulted in his inability to play basketball this year. The therapist asked Farooq, "So what kept you going?" "My belief in

Allah," Farooq replied. He also took feelings of comfort and strength from the Koran and the story of Job in particular.

In addition, sometimes Farooq struggled with cultural conflict: He wanted to maintain his Islamic beliefs and practices; at the same time, there were multiple temptations on his college campus. When he drank alcohol at parties, Farooq felt especially guilty. What helped him most then? "Remembering Allah's forgiveness," Farooq answered. Abu Raiya and Pargament suggested normalizing the struggle. The strategic solution focused therapist providing input to Farooq at the end of the session might say something like this: "I'm not surprised you struggle with your faith. It's not easy caring so deeply about your values and at the same time knowing that music and a few drinks are part of the world you live in. I'm impressed that you know that your deep wish to not offend Allah helps you through the darkest times. It lets you know that when you think about taking your life, Allah has commanded you to be patient, and you remember Allah's immense capacity for forgiveness. And when the deep sadness comes up again, which you know that it may, because you know Allah sometimes tests you, you will remember all this, and notice how it makes a difference."

Tou, a 37-year-old Laotian man, was referred by his psychiatrist for "anxiety management techniques." Tou had been on psychiatric disability for many years. He lived with his mother, and he spoke English, Chinese, and Laotian. Tou described feelings of panic, which occurred when the TV "taunted" him for being Laotian. Tou saw images and heard voices, and it felt to him "like being raped." His best hopes were for the panic to go away. What would let Tou know that the panic was diminishing? Not hearing the voices, he said, especially the ones that were in English. When were the voices less of a problem? When texting or surfing the Internet, Tou said. It also helped when he talked back to the voices, in Laotian. What was the worst thing that a therapist might recommend? "ECT [electroconvulsive shock therapy]," Tou replied immediately. "That would really feel like rape." What would be the best thing? "Some ideas to calm me down." What was a special thing about Tou? "I like to speak my native language, Laotian," he said.

Then Tou added that sometimes he questions whether he is straight or gay. Most of the time he is unsure. The therapist wondered aloud whether Tou's questioning is associated with the "feeling of being raped." The therapist added that, as strange as it may seem, American sex therapists sometimes encourage people to enjoy multiple sexual fantasies.

The therapist asked Tou if he would like to create a list together of things that might calm him down. They would take turns generating possibilities. Tou liked the idea of doing this. Here is the list they made together: cooking, taking his medicine, mowing the lawn, getting "back to real," thinking about the pomegranate tree in the back yard, talking back to the voices (in English or Laotian), Chinese and English music, tea, coffee, turning the TV off, telling the voices that he doesn't have to do what they say, thinking that it's okay to not be sure if he is gay or straight or "bi," walking, going to the gym, cutting his old jeans into cutoffs, remembering that sexual fantasies are normal, spending time with his dog, checking his investments on the computer, and talking to his mom.

Tou said that he felt less anxious after making this list. The therapist complimented him on recognizing that so many different things can help and invited him to select tools from his list—and to add new ones to it. When asked what he wanted to remember from his appointment, Tou said, "You're a nice person, and you helped me realize that fantasies are okay." After the session, the therapist reflected on the many ways in which this session was different from what the referring psychiatrist probably had in mind for Tou.

The following two clients are women who, on one level, share a cultural background. Both were born in Mexico and moved to California in childhood with their families. Both are in their middle 50s. Both are divorced, with adult children. However, there are also significant and important differences between them, in the domains of education, occupation, nature of the complaint, psychiatric history, strengths, support systems, and the meaning of their Hispanic heritage.

Esperanza was referred for an appointment by the psychiatrist who prescribed her antipsychotic medication. She came to the session accompanied by her friend, Maria. What were Esperanza's best hopes from coming here? She wanted a "clear mind." What would let her know that was beginning to happen? She would "feel calm inside." Were any pieces of this already happening? Yes. Maria was stopping by, helping her to remember to take her medicine. Sometimes Maria massaged her back. That made "a world of difference." What else helped Esperanza? Keeping busy, she said. How did she do that? Watering her flowers helped her. Cooking was very helpful, too. Sometimes she made enchiladas. Her ex-husband had a food truck, and she used to help him. Putting her pills in a little box, with a section for each day of the week, helped her, too. The box was like a beautiful carved wooden box that Esperanza had as a little girl. The session ended with the therapist encouraging Esperanza to continue to use that box, to nurture her flowers, to cook, and to make some enchiladas for Maria. Maria smiled a broad smile at that suggestion. At the end of the session, Esperanza thanked the therapist. She said, "You are a nice lady. Your presence calms me. And your sweater is very pretty."

Soledad was self-referred. A professor of film studies, she wanted to establish a relationship with a therapist. Soledad wanted to live more honestly, with both passion and balance. Her immediate concern was the hard time she had saying "no," especially to a difficult colleague. Soledad's cultural background was of special importance to her. She said, "I feel privileged to be able to address social justice issues in my work: race, class, gender, sexual orientation. I knew I could do it in the Latino community, but to be able to do it with white kids, kids of privilege—I'm blessed beyond my dreams." Students sometimes told her that she had opened their eyes to multiculturalism. Soledad loved to read novels about different cultures and was working on a screenplay.

Soledad had been helped immensely by a therapist 20 years ago. She said, "She was wise. She cried with me, she validated what I've been through, and she told me that what I've been through informs who I am now. She made me feel like I have a right to feel this way."

The therapist and Soledad talked about how the difficult colleague she encountered now was similar in both appearance and personality to an aunt who had criticized both Soledad and her mother. Soledad had often disagreed with the aunt, but she was not allowed to discuss her feelings with anyone. It made sense that it was hard for Soledad to be appropriately assertive with someone who reminded her of her aunt in multiple ways. There was discussion of how Soledad would probably feel awkward setting limits—and sometimes would do so anyway. The therapist invited Soledad to think of herself as a multifaceted and loveable protagonist in a wonderful screenplay. Soledad was also encouraged to savor the next semester, when her colleague would be on sabbatical. When asked what she wanted to remember from the session, Soledad responded, "Your question of what worked to survive with my aunt. I never thought about it that way before."

The reader may remember that Carmen, the client discussed in Chapters 5 and 6 in this book, is of Hispanic background. Carmen's parents came to the United States from Mexico when Carmen was a child. Carmen occasionally speaks Spanish to her mother, but she mostly speaks English. The family name for Carmen's mom is Lita, an abbreviation of *abuelita* (grandmother in Spanish). At several points during the therapy, the therapist wondered aloud with Carmen about how much the mom's perceived dependence on Carmen—and Carmen's feelings of guilt when setting limits—were connected to their cultural background. Carmen consistently said that she did not feel that the cultural component was primary. Carmen's "position" was that her mom had the language, education, and degree of acculturation to function adequately in the community. For Carmen, alcoholism—and Mom's regression because of her relapses—were the primary explanatory factors. The therapist took into account the cultural factors, but the most important considerations were Carmen's view of these and respecting Carmen's position.

ETHICAL ISSUES IN SOLUTION-FOCUSED AND STRATEGIC THERAPY

Psychotherapists of all disciplines and of all orientations have legal and ethical codes to uphold. They need to maintain confidentiality, obtain informed consent, and protect the rights, well-being, and safety of their clients, the general public, the organizations they serve, and themselves. They must avoid conflicts of interest and refrain from working outside their areas of competence. Sperry (2010a) noted that therapists may approach ethics in three ways. The first perspective, which represents a lower level of competency in this domain, emphasizes enforcement of rules. The second level, which exists between the first and the third, emphasizes compliance while including more reflection about the principles. At the third and highest level, the therapist integrates professional ethics with his or her personal ethics and life philosophy. There is increased sensitivity to subtle ethical issues, with greater ability to anticipate and articulate potential dilemmas and conflicts of interest before they occur. As a result, therapists at this level may be better able to prevent problems and to address them when they do arise.

Some therapists may think of ethics primarily as guidelines that "tell therapists what *not* to do." In contrast, a perspective described as "positive ethics" (Knapp & VanDeCreek, 2006) considers doing the greatest good. This is an aspirational view, consistent with the solution-focused attitudes emphasized throughout this book. Positive ethics support the therapist

150

in knowing legal and ethical principles and maintaining them, not just because one is legally bound to do so but because one is striving to do what is right for the client and the larger good.

Here is an example of a dilemma involving boundaries and confidentiality. While enjoying himself with friends at a football game, the therapist noticed, a few rows back, a female client whom he had seen for the first time earlier that week. He could not tell if she had seen him. He immediately turned away. He felt anxious. He did not want to violate his client's confidentiality, and he knew that if he waved or said "Hi," his friends would ask who that attractive woman was. The therapist made a point of not looking over his shoulder throughout the game. He had a feeling that his client had, in fact, seen him, because he was only a few rows in front of her. She returned the following week, and the therapist made no mention of seeing her. The client also did not refer to it, that day or ever. The therapist will never know if she saw him or if she suspected that he had deliberately avoided acknowledging her. But he had a feeling that the encounter—and his handling of it—limited the quality of the therapeutic alliance throughout their work together.

How might a therapist at a higher level of competency in this area have responded in this situation? He might have processed his own reaction and considered how he would respond if he said hello and his friends did ask him who that was. He could say "Someone I know from work" and leave it at that. Then, when it was natural to turn, if their glances met, he would smile and wave. Football—and spirit for the home team—might become part of the language of therapy.

Let us also consider how the therapist who said nothing at the game might react if he later regretted his choice, sensing that it was negatively impacting the therapeutic relationship. He might acknowledge that he had seen his client and had wanted to protect her confidentiality but later had sensed that he might have come across as rude, as if he were avoiding her. They could process this together. Acknowledging fallibility and being able to talk openly about the relationship can strengthen the therapeutic alliance. It offers an example of "doing what works" both in the therapeutic alliance and in other relationships in most people's lives.

In the following example, the therapist sensed that Leah, a new client, seemed vaguely familiar but could not say why. When asked to describe something special about herself, Leah's face lit up. "I love bonsai trees," she said. Later in the session, Leah said that she would know that her depression was lifting when she returned to nurturing her little trees. The

151

therapist had a flash of recognition. She, too, was a bonsai enthusiast, and she belonged to the local Bonsai Society. She now recalled that Leah had attended one meeting of the society about 6 months earlier. The therapist immediately considered whether it was a conflict of interest to see Leah. Not only was the therapist an active member of the society; she also hosted its annual holiday gathering at her home. Leah was not specifically talking about returning to the Bonsai Society. Nevertheless, she obviously knew that it existed. The therapist decided to tell Leah that she recognized her from that meeting. She asked Leah if it felt like a conflict of interest to work together. Leah did not think so. She wanted only a few sessions. They agreed that if it ever felt uncomfortable for either of them, either could bring it up.

Leah returned. Occasionally the therapist used tree imagery, which Leah understood and built on. After a few sessions, Leah said she felt better, and she was ready to discontinue regular appointments for now. The understanding was that she could return, either for an occasional booster session or for a series of appointments, if desired.

Several months later, Leah began to attend Bonsai Society meetings semiregularly. The therapist and Leah always greeted each other. They talked about plants and gardens, as all members did, but nothing more personal. Leah did not attend the holiday party but continued to attend many (but not all) meetings, and over the next year she became an active participant in the society.

Then one day the therapist saw Leah's name on her schedule. By now she felt that she *did* have a relationship with Leah through their shared hobby. The therapist considered calling Leah to discuss this on the phone but decided against it. Instead, she shared her dilemma with a trusted colleague. She decided she would allow Leah to keep the appointment. She would see what Leah was wanting at this point, and they would discuss this together. Leah was now experiencing some guilt about a recent interaction with her father, and she wanted a few sessions to discuss that relationship. The therapist told Leah that at this point, it seemed like it would be more helpful for Leah to see a different therapist. Leah said that she was a little disappointed but that she understood. She was also a little relieved, because it felt somewhat awkward for her, too. Fortunately, there were many excellent therapists available at the clinic, and a successful transfer of care was arranged. Had the presenting concern been one where this therapist was the only professional in the community with expertise in the area of concern, the situation would have been more complicated. Again, anticipating dilemmas, consulting with colleagues, and talking openly are important ingredients of the solution.

The following example illustrates how a trainee who was learning solution-focused and strategic methods approached a different kind of dilemma. Her client, Jason, had been referred for treatment of "social phobia." The therapist had recently learned some strategic and solution-focused techniques for treating social anxiety and was eager to try them out. However, when asked about his best hopes from treatment, Jason indicated that he wanted to sort out how much his depression was "biological or stress related."

Jason had taken medication for depression and anxiety off and on for many years, and he believed that exploring this issue in more depth would help him to make an educated decision about whether to begin a conversation with his psychiatrist about getting off medicine completely. Jason described himself as a quiet person, with only a few friends. People in his life (and most recently the physician who referred him for this appointment) had repeatedly told him that he needs to be more social, but in that area, Jason was comfortable as he was.

Jason's therapist recognized a feeling of disappointment. Although she had hoped to suggest experiments like "Pretend that you are the second shyest person in the room and look for someone shyer than you are," doing so at this point would be meeting *her* needs more than Jason's. Listening to what Jason wanted and building on that, the therapist asked instead how Jason would know that he was building his understanding. The session ended with Jason deciding to notice the times when he felt depressed or anxious and what he did to help the medicine (which he was already taking) to work. The therapist discussed this in supervision, reflecting that she had actually learned something more valuable than using a new tool: the convergence of professional ethics, personal ethics, and the all-important solution-focused and strategic attitude of respecting and following the client.

THE COUNTERINTUITIVE: "EMPATHY, NOT TRICKERY"

As Quick (2008) pointed out, interventions that include counterintuitive or paradoxical suggestions to clients—as some strategic and strategic solution focused approaches do—have sometimes been criticized for being "manipulative." She noted that Cade and O'Hanlon (1993) described paradoxical methods as "empathy, not trickery." They wrote:

> It is our view that what have previously been termed paradoxical strategies have the effect of empowering clients through the process of acknowledging their perfectly valid cautious, more fearful concerns about change and leaving them to operate out of their own arguments as to why change should be attempted. (p. 157)

Discussing the use of the counterintuitive in the blended strategic solution focused model, Quick directly addressed potential concerns about ethical questions or trickery:

> [I]n strategic solution focused therapy, second-order messages with a "paradoxical" flavor are emphatically not trickery or gimmicks designed "behind the client's back." Just the opposite is true: in this approach, any message that includes a counterintuitive component emerges from a collaborative discussion. Often there is consideration of universal existential realities about dilemmas and feelings that may not be fully changeable. (p. 96)

Within the context of a collaborative therapist–client relationship, strategic solution focused therapists may directly comment on this process. For example, the therapist might say, "I'm very aware right now that you're here because you want to stop *X*, and here we are talking about deliberately creating *X*, and in a way how weird that is, maybe just the opposite of what you thought we would be doing in here." This kind of comment invites the client to discuss and process this component of the therapy.

It should also be emphasized that doing what works emphatically does not mean inviting clients to manipulate or take advantage of others in order to meet their short-term needs. Doing what works is discussed on multiple levels. As described in several examples in this book (including the Melody and Christine examples in Chapter 4), strategic solution focused therapists may actively point out that something that works in the short run may *not* work in the long run or at another level. This is especially the case if a behavior violates legal or ethical standards or threatens the rights or dignity of others.

The therapist may model acknowledgement and discussion of mixed feelings when these emerge. For example, a therapist recognizes during a session that a report to Child Protective Services is needed. The client is attempting to persuade the therapist not to make the call. The therapist might say something like this: "I'm very aware right now that you really don't want me make that phone call I just mentioned and that I have to do it anyway. And, I want to tell you: There's a part of me that wishes that I could just pretend that I didn't know what you just told me. But I *do* know it now, and I know that both you and I have to tolerate the discomfort we feel with my having to make that report." That combination of "tolerating discomfort and doing it anyway" is a powerful component of a doing what works approach in many situations. Therefore, the highly competent therapist's ability to recognize, verbalize, and share this experience in a difficult situation becomes an "ingredient of the solution" on multiple levels.

11

Becoming a Highly Effective and Competent Solution-Focused and Strategic Therapist

This chapter describes optimal competency-based training that fosters highly effective practice beyond the *minimum competency* level; that is, at the *proficient* level of expertise and higher. It discusses how therapists at different stages of competency approach the knowledge, skill, and attitude components of the solution-focused and strategic therapies, with examples of different levels of competency. The chapter also describes some methods for moving to higher levels of competency. At the higher levels of solution-focused and strategic practice, therapists more quickly and intuitively recognize when something is not working for this client at this point in therapy. They listen carefully to their clients. They are flexible and creative, combining conceptual, procedural, and reflective information in new ways. The chapter introduces some specific solution-focused strategies that may be used in training programs, clinical supervision, and/or self-reflection, inviting therapists to embrace challenges, increase flexibility, and transform impasses into interactions that make a difference in their clients' lives.

HOW COMPETENCY GROWS

Other chapters in this book have described in some detail *what* therapists do at different levels of competency. This chapter addresses *how* therapists can increase their proficiency, or the *process* of growing as a therapist. As noted in Chapter 1, levels of proficiency include novice, advanced beginner, competent, proficient, and expert, and declarative, procedural, and reflective learning all support movement to higher levels.

At any level, progression to the next stage is supported by respectful, collaborative interpersonal relationships. As Kaslow (2004) pointed out, the same kind of collaborative relationships and attitudes that are so important for clients also facilitate therapist development. McKergow (2010) has suggested that expertise in solution-focused practice—and solution-focused attitudes in particular—may grow from the experience of receiving solution-focused supervision or coaching. One can learn many solution-focused tools in a brief training, but the collaborative relationship may be incorporated best from experiencing it. Although the solution-focused and strategic approaches do not require "personal therapy to resolve old issues" as a prerequisite for competent practice, working with solution-focused colleagues, supervisors, and mentors can be an extremely powerful "ingredient of the solution" for amplifying proficiency.

Kaslow (2004) has also noted that training should include didactic, experiential, and mentoring components, with sequences of progressively more complex methods and content. She emphasized the value of working alongside a mentor and of role-playing vignettes (with feedback from peers and/or supervisors or consultants). Reading and learning about new developments in one's field feed curiosity and growth. Feedback from multiple informants (peers, clients, and supervisors), sometimes called *360-degree assessment*, provides useful information for ongoing professional development. Self-assessment, through formal scales or ongoing self-reflection, also plays a valuable role.

Trainees and staff who are beginning new jobs often receive some of this support automatically (whether they want it or not). In contrast, therapists who are already licensed usually need to take far more initiative in creating and maintaining systems that will provide this kind of stimulation. After licensure, some therapists are relieved that the training process is complete and seek little additional input. Those therapists who actively seek out continuing stimulation and feedback are more likely to grow in

158

proficiency. Sperry (2010a) has commented that being a psychotherapist can be viewed as a job, a career, or a calling. One might hypothesize that those therapists who see the work more as a calling seek out and participate in more of the activities described above.

As described in Chapter 1, competency includes knowledge, skills, and attitudes, three components that are interrelated and at the same time distinct. *Knowledge* refers to the conceptual foundation that guides one's practice. It grows from formal training, including reading and study. *Skills*, or procedures, are the therapeutic methods. They are learned from study, observation, and repeated practice, ideally with feedback, both from clients and supervisors. *Attitudes* are values and feelings toward the work and the people involved. Attitudes can be described explicitly during training; they can also be implicit, and therapists can observe the attitudes communicated by their mentors and their peers. The following sections provide examples of therapists at different levels of competency in each of the three components, and they offer some ideas about how to move to higher levels.

KNOWLEDGE AT DIFFERENT LEVELS OF PROFICIENCY

The following vignette illustrates an extremely low level of knowledge about solution-focused and strategic practice. Brie is a marriage and family therapy trainee who expresses interest in doing strategic solution focused work at her new placement. She said, "I actually think I already use that approach." When asked to describe an example of her work, Brie described a case where "I helped the client to come up with a practical solution to his procrastination by suggesting that he go to the library. I didn't focus a lot on his past or his childhood or anything like that. I gave him a strategy to use, a specific solution."

Not every approach that includes the word *solution* or *strategy* is solution-focused or strategic! Brie did not recognize this. Learning about the history, assumptions, and theory of the solution-focused and strategic approaches could introduce Brie to the models and would be one important component of beginning to do solution-focused or strategic work. Reading and study alone are not sufficient, but they provide a good start.

Therapists often have differing degrees of knowledge about different domains within their professions. Juliana is a licensed psychologist who completed her PhD about 10 years ago. She was trained in solution-focused and other strength-based approaches, and when she conducts therapy (which she does about 4 hours each week), she still uses those methods. But Juliana's true professional passion is learning disability evaluation of adults. Whenever there is an opportunity to do more testing, she eagerly does so. She avidly follows the literature on educational assessment and attends and presents at conferences on the topic. She rarely reads anything about solution-focused or strategic practice. Recently a psychology graduate student asked Juliana about the assumptions of systemic practice, and Juliana acknowledged that she did not really know what they were. (As a responsible psychologist, she knew where to look for the information, and she e-mailed the student the response to his question the next day.) Although highly proficient in her knowledge of learning disability assessment, Juliana is only minimally competent in her knowledge about solution-focused and strategic practice.

Eduardo completed his PhD around the same time that Juliana did. Solution-focused therapy is his professional passion. He regularly reads articles and books on the subject and attends solution-focused therapy conferences and trainings whenever he can. Every year Eduardo presents a series of seminars on solution-focused practices to interns at his agency. He looks forward to reviewing his notes before the seminars. "I feel like I'm connecting with my roots," Eduardo said. "I also think my therapy is better after the seminars, because I'm reminding myself of the conceptual foundation. What I do isn't simply a random set of techniques." Eduardo is thinking about writing an article on the theoretical underpinnings of solution-focused practice. Although Eduardo would not consider himself an expert, his grasp of theory and knowledge places him at a level of high proficiency in this domain.

The activities that Eduardo enjoys can help a therapist at any level of proficiency to enhance his or her grasp of the conceptual foundation. Reading basic texts and recent literature in the field and attending conferences and workshops all add to declarative learning. Teaching the basic concepts to others and pointing out the connections between theory, technique, and attitude not only pass along declarative learning to others, they also reinforce the teacher's fundamental assumptions. "Going slow," remembering that solutions are not necessarily related to problems, and building on unique client characteristics are among "the basics," and one cannot return to them too often.

SKILLS AT DIFFERENT LEVELS OF PROFICIENCY

Skills at the beginner or advanced beginner level are demonstrated by Tom, a marriage and family counselor, 8 years post-master's. Tom has recently begun to practice solution-focused therapy and is very excited about it. However, sometimes he becomes so focused on "doing it the right way," asking all the right questions, in the right order, that he forgets to truly listen. Instead of being solution-focused, Tom becomes "solution forced" (Nylund & Corsiglia, 1994). Often he fails to recognize that a client is feeling "pressured" to come up with exceptions. Tom often asks miracle questions prematurely, without waiting for the opportunity for such questions to emerge naturally from the conversation. When his clients do not give the answers he expects, or when they want to ventilate about their pain, Tom feels confused. He then starts to doubt the solution-focused process, and sometimes he abandons it.

The next example illustrates skills that have recently grown from the advanced beginner stage to a stage of minimal or adequate competency, with a strong desire to move to a higher level. Amanda is completing her predoctoral internship at an agency where she has done a great deal of solution-focused and strategic therapy, and she has been excited by the approaches. "This way of working makes so much sense," she says.

> It truly fits who I am as a therapist, and it's exciting to see my clients making so many changes so quickly. I've loved our seminars where we observe each other through the one-way mirror. It's like exercising a muscle, like I'm feeling my skills grow stronger.

Next year Amanda will be working in a different setting, and to her knowledge, there will not be structured opportunities to observe strategic or solution-focused practice. "I'll miss what we had here," Amanda says to her supervisor. "I want to learn to use these tools at a more sophisticated level and with more complex cases." She wants to brainstorm ways of making this happen.

Amanda's supervisor is David, a tenured professor of psychology who in recent years has spent more time doing teaching, research, and supervision, with fewer hours of direct client care each week. David shared with Amanda that he too strives to retain—and continue to develop and fine-tune—his skills as a strategic solution focused therapist. He told Amanda that he often has wondered: "How can I effectively teach my

161

students to do strategic solution focused therapy if I'm not actively doing it myself?"

David talked with Amanda about the concept of deliberate practice, which involves actively seeking out activities designed to improve specific aspects of an ability. He remembered reading an interview with Insoo Kim Berg in which Berg was asked what she thought therapists needed to do to become seasoned and skilled therapists. Berg identified several core components. One was repeated practice: "Just keep doing it, doing it, doing it. Like a pianist, for hours and hours and hours. ... I tell you, we did that for years. I think that's what it takes" (Yalom & Rubin, 2010). David had been thinking how similar this concept is to what Ericsson (2000) has called "the 10,000 hour rule." Experts in many fields differ from people at moderate levels of proficiency in terms of the number of hours they have spent at their craft. Experience alone does not produce proficiency, but it is one important component, and Amanda would have many opportunities to practice during the coming year.

David described some of the ways he looks for and creates opportunities to sharpen his skills. He regularly attends conferences and workshops that feature hands-on practice. He appreciates opportunities for direct observation of master therapists, both live and on video.[1]

David told Amanda how he had looked for a peer consultation group in his area, and when he could not find one, he created an informal one. Once a month, a small group of solution-focused and strategic therapists meets for case sharing, reflection, and a sense of community. Although they do not have the luxury of observing each other through a one-way mirror, sometimes they "pretend" that they have one. Sometimes they imagine that experts with diverse perspectives are offering their thoughts: "What would Insoo Kim Berg (or John Weakland, or any other mentor or role model, living or dead) be suggesting right now?" "What would a 'pure' strategic therapist be recommending?" "What would a 'pure' solution-focused therapist say?" The "purists" in the group (both strategic and solution-focused) reflect on what the integrative approach would emphasize. They sometimes "invite" guests from other orientations for a hypothetical consult. What would a wise cognitive behavioral or psychodynamic therapist be recommending?

David also shared his conviction that his best teachers are his clients and that asking for feedback continues to be of immense value in the growth of his clinical skills. When something has not worked well enough,

David also reflects on his own about what is working and what is not. When "problem clarifying isn't clarifying" or "miracle questions aren't creating miracles" (Quick, 2008), he thinks about how to shift stances and how he might do something different.

During the conversation with Amanda, David remembered a tool he learned from Freeman (2010). Adapted from Dolan's (1998) "letter from the future" exercise, this tool is called "an e-mail from the future." This exercise invites the therapist to imagine that it is a year (or other interval) later, and he or she is reflecting on the ways that proficiency has grown and how this change happened. Amanda was able to describe how she would be "practicing like a pianist does," leading from behind, reflecting, and creating opportunities for consultation and support online and in her new community. Amanda noted that she would also be remembering the many ideas she had learned from David, a role model who created and maintained skills at the highly proficient level.

ATTITUDES AT DIFFERENT LEVELS OF PROFICIENCY

The following example illustrates attitudes that are not consistent with solution-focused or strategic practice. Fred recently completed his master's in social work and began a new job at an agency where several staff members use strategic methods. He immediately let his manager know that he had received some training in strategic therapy and that this was an area of interest for him. "I'm really good with the counterintuitive," Fred added.

Fred's supervisor (who, fortunately, was an experienced strategic therapist) soon began to have some concerns about Fred's attitude. Fred talked about "how cool this reverse psychology thing is." Sometimes he seemed flippant and condescending. Once Fred said, "I tell just about everyone to keep having their symptoms." The chart notes showed that Fred frequently ended sessions with suggestions that had a paradoxical or counterintuitive component. Often there was little in the note—or in what Fred described in supervision—to indicate that the suggestions were being individually tailored to clients' unique characteristics.

The supervisor also learned that far too many of Fred's clients were not returning. In addition, too many were calling the clinic to request a transfer to a different therapist. They often said that they just had not felt a connection with Fred. The supervisor quickly recognized that Fred's work was not meeting minimal standards of competency. Fred's attitude was reflected in his intervention planning and delivery. What he was doing was not working for his clients. And it was not working for Fred either, because his job might soon be in jeopardy.

Remembering and building upon Fred's appreciation for the strategic approach, the supervisor considered how to discuss his concerns with Fred. He wanted to do so in a way that conveyed the core strategic attitude of respect for Fred and what he cared about. Gently but clearly, the supervisor suggested that Fred's approach had unwittingly become an unsuccessful attempted solution. They talked about ways of going back to the basic attitudes and methods of a strategic approach, including respect, refusal to pathologize, careful observation of what is unique about someone, and taking a conversational, one-down position during sessions. In the spirit of "going slow," Fred might not yet know by the end of a session what would make the biggest difference in someone's life. He could acknowledge that openly, while also inviting his client to notice what was different about the complaint between now and next time.

As Fred began to do this, he discovered with great precision how his clients' complaints were problematic. He also learned fascinating things about his clients that had nothing whatsoever to do with their problems. He increasingly let his clients know that it made sense that they reacted as they did. With his droll, low-key sense of humor, Fred was increasingly connecting with his clients. Now, when Fred made counterintuitive suggestions, these grew from a deeper understanding of client position, and suggestions were made in the context of a therapeutic alliance. It soon became clear that Fred was absolutely correct: He *did* have a creative ability to discover and use the counterintuitive. When he did so in a way that reflected the core attitudes of strategic therapy, his competency grew significantly.

In the next example, the therapist recognizes that she is struggling to maintain a solution-focused attitude. Suzanne is a seasoned therapist, well respected by her peers. She has been practicing for more than 20 years, and she considers her primary model to be strategic solution focused. It has been a number of years since Suzanne's training, and she readily acknowledges she has experienced some "drift" away from some of the core attitudes of strategic solution focused therapy. Most of her colleagues emphasize the importance of traditional diagnosis and psychopathology, and most take an expert stance. Suzanne said,

> When a patient—listen to me, I've even started calling my clients "patients," like people do around here—comes back saying that the miracle is actually happening, sometimes I find myself wondering, like my colleagues always do, "Is he getting hypomanic?" And this isn't because he's irritable, or talking fast, or not sleeping, or anything like that, but just because he's telling me all these amazing things that he's doing. Or when someone is drinking but not defining it as a problem, I start forgetting that people are really the experts on what they want to change and when they're ready to do it. I really do need an attitude tune up!

Hearing an update on solution-focused and strategic practice recently reminded Suzanne how easy it was to slide away from the attitudes she truly valued. She did some reflection and journaling on her own, and she thought about where she could get support from like-minded therapists.

Latisha works at a community clinic. After an introduction to solution-focused practice a few years ago at a mandatory training sponsored by her agency, Latisha instantly recognized that "this approach is why I went into this field. This is what I have been waiting for." Latisha listens attentively to all her clients. She takes delight in discovering their hidden strengths and interesting details about their lives. With gentle humor, she repeatedly conveys her deep belief that current troubles are never the most interesting thing about someone.

Latisha would love to get more training in solution-focused practice. "But, hey, I'm a single mom. I barely keep my kids in flip flops. I don't have the money to go off to those solution-focused conferences," she says. She is not at all hesitant to acknowledge that she is jealous of colleagues who have the luxury of getting more training—and sometimes in places she has only dreamed of visiting. But Latisha is not waiting for that kind of training in order to deepen her solution focus. She has discovered a solution-focused Internet discussion group. At first she only read what others wrote, but recently she has begun contributing to it as well. Latisha says, "It is so awesome to see the strength and resilience that people have. It's like a treasure hunt. I know the treasure is in there somewhere, and that people are going to discover it."

Like David, Latisha uses her solution-focused attitudes with colleagues as well as clients. When there are conflicts in the workplace, she says, "Okay, girlfriend, when this is behind us, what will you and I be laughing about?" Latisha's knowledge and skills (which are still growing) may currently be at the level of adequate competency, but her attitude suggests proficiency at a significantly higher level.

As noted in the case examples described throughout this chapter, reflection—about both what is working and what is not—is a basic and critical tool. Do patterns emerge in the feedback I receive? What is different when things go well (ratings of alliance, client outcome, something else)? When clients are not benefiting, what is different? What are my clients telling me? (And do I ask them how I can be more helpful? If I do not ask them, they will not tell me!) What do I do to get back on track?

A specific type of reflection has been suggested by a therapist who observed that she sometimes did especially good work with clients she *disliked* (A. Groves, personal communication, Spring, 1982). This was because recognition of her own reactions led her to use extra effort to empathize with these clients and to communicate caring to them. It is also important to be especially careful with a client whom one actively *likes* or to whom one feels similar. Reflecting on one's own, in supervision, or with colleagues, the therapist might consider: What might I be missing—or focusing on too closely—because of my own reactions? If I had "just an ordinary reaction" to this person, what might I do differently? What is my initial, gut-level idea of what to say to this person? What is the main message I have been giving? How would the client answer that question? What would be the *opposite* of that response? The purpose of this exercise is *not* to suggest that therapists automatically change what they are doing. Rather, the idea is to reflect and to consider.

PREVENTING BURNOUT: HEALING INVOLVEMENT VERSUS STRESSFUL INVOLVEMENT

What differentiates therapists who become more proficient over time from those who "burn out" over time? Some research conducted by Orlinsky and Rønnestad (2005) sheds some light on this question. After analyzing detailed reports from 5,000 therapists from many countries, these authors identified two factors: *healing involvement*, which referred to positive experience, a kind of "flow" when working with clients, and *stressful involvement*, which included boredom and anxiety during sessions. Three variables were associated with healing involvement. First, there was a sense of "cumulative career development"; second, there was "theoretical breadth" (this referred to the use of multiple theoretical perspectives); and third, there was a sense of "currently experienced growth." Experiential learning, through direct client contact and learning from one's clients, was a significant factor in therapist growth and development.

One might ask: How can a solution-focused, strategic, or strategic solution focused therapist follow the model and also have "theoretical breadth" in clinical work? The strategic solution focused therapist, of course, is already using an integrated model. In addition, as discussed in Chapters 6 and 7, highly effective solution-focused and strategic therapists do integrate other tools into their work. In the spirit of building on what the client brings, if a client believes that a particular approach can be helpful, that approach can become an ingredient of the solution. For example, a client tells her therapist that she would like to better understand her dreams, because she thinks that her unconscious mind is trying to tell her something, maybe warning her about something. Let us imagine that her therapist is Tom, the therapist described above who sometimes becomes "solution forced" (Nylund & Corsiglia, 1994) and who on other occasions abandons a solution-focused approach prematurely. How might Tom proceed?

When the client brings up the subject of dreams, Tom's initial, gut-level reaction might be one of defensiveness and irritation. Basically changing the subject, he might try to pursue a standard miracle question. Or he might abandon any attempts to continue therapy during the session, focusing instead on referring the client to another therapist. Tom might feel inadequate, annoyed at the client, or concerned about "concealing" from a supervisor that the client's presenting concerns did not "fit the model."

Now let us imagine that the therapist is David, the therapist described above whose skills (and knowledge and attitudes) approach the expert level of proficiency. David might be curious about the dream that the client would like to understand. Why is this of interest now? What has helped the client to understand and use her dreams in the past? If the session is helpful in just the way she wants, and the dream guides her just as she hopes it will, how will that show? Where will the client embrace appropriate caution, proceeding slowly, because of some inner wisdom? Where will she feel freer to take action? David might feel energized by the opportunity to create a new variation on a miracle question or a strategic "restraint from change" perspective that emerges from what the client brings. He might reflect on how different models approach—or ignore—dreams. That reflection might lead to a stimulating discussion with a colleague, a conversation in a peer review group, an idea for a research project or journal article, or a presentation at a conference. To use Orlinsky

167

and Rønnestad's (2005) term, David's healing involvement with this client might facilitate client goal attainment and simultaneously enhance proficiency within the therapist—and it might invite some valuable discussion and thinking in the professional community.

ENHANCING COMPETENCY IN SOLUTION-FOCUSED AND STRATEGIC WORK: ADDITIONAL THOUGHTS, METHODS, AND EXERCISES

As seen in the examples above, highly effective solution-focused and strategic therapists repeatedly return to the core concepts, methods, and attitudes introduced in Chapter 2 and elaborated throughout this book. Not knowing; being curious, surprised, and flexible; seeking and welcoming feedback; discovering what works and changing what does not: All of these comprise "the basics." Again, one cannot return to them too often.

One simple but powerful way of returning to the basics is "having a first session again," especially if therapy is not working well enough. Some seasoned therapists have commented that although they certainly try to listen carefully and use their tools in any session, they listen most carefully and use their tools more precisely during a first session. If this is the case, then the therapist can act as if this is the first session again.

Although it may seem like a "no-brainer" that therapists should review their notes and remind themselves of what has worked in the past and what has not, in busy practice settings, this may not happen consistently. The author and her trainees have sometimes discovered that chart review, in preparation for a case presentation or some other purpose, reminds the therapist of important strengths and solutions. Reviewing the record with the client is sometimes even more helpful than reviewing it alone or with a colleague.

Conducting microanalysis of one's own sessions is another tool that solution-focused therapists sometimes use to obtain feedback about the details of how they use language. For example, one might learn from this process how frequently one uses the client's own words in formulations and whether this emphasis usually follows positive or negative client utterances. The patterns observed can be compared with those seen in microanalyses of sessions conducted by "master" solution-focused therapists. Bavelas, Gerwing, Healing, and Tomori (2010) have offered training in this kind of microanalysis.

Building on some of the lessons learned through microanalysis, Smock (2010) has used the following method for solution-focused individual supervision. Prior to supervision, the therapist is asked to select a 5-minute segment of a video that he or she particularly likes. As the supervisor and the supervisee watch it together, the supervisor develops a list of specific change-facilitating things that the supervisee is doing. Variables such as tone, phrasing, timing, inflection, and posture are noted as well as content. Together the supervisor and supervisee notice what preceded and followed these therapist responses and discover ways to build on what works.

Smock (2010) raised this excellent question: What if the supervisee selects a segment that, in the supervisor's opinion, is *not* particularly solution-focused? This scenario is especially likely to happen with therapists who are in the beginning stages of competency. Here, the supervisor looks for the moments when the therapist *starts* to display the behaviors and attitudes of solution-focused practice. These are highlighted, with discussion of how one could make them even *more* solution-focused. Smock emphasizes the importance of communicating to trainees that this fine-tuning is not something done only by beginners. Rather, the process of identifying successes and building on what works enhances solution-focused practice at all levels of proficiency.

J. Simon (2010) has introduced a method called "When the client doesn't follow the script." This tool acknowledges that when clients give unpredictable responses, it is all too easy for therapists to forget the tools and attitudes of accepting, respecting, and utilizing people's unique ways of cooperating. This exercise offers a number of brief scenarios that most therapists will find challenging. Here are some examples (pp. 215–216):

Therapist: When you wake up, how will you know this miracle happened?
Client: I never sleep.

Therapist: So what will tell you our time together is done?
Client: Done? Are you dumping me? Already?

Therapist: On a scale from 0 to 10 … where would you put yourself?
Client: Oh, right now? I'm at a 15!

Therapist: Let's suppose that our meeting together is helpful to you. How will you know …?
Client: I'm glad you asked me. The space aliens would stop following me.

As therapists role-play these scenarios, they discover and create solution-focused interventions in an atmosphere of safety, spontaneity, and fun.

Examples like the above quickly lead therapists to share their own scenarios—each a kind of "worst message question" for therapists. As mentioned in Chapter 4, Gorden (2010b) described a method that invites therapists to generate their "worst fears" of what a client could say. "You suck," "You obviously don't care about me," and "I am really attracted to you right now" are some of the responses that Gorden addresses. Brainstorming these scenarios helps to address transference and countertransference reactions from a solution-focused and/or strategic perspective.

Wheeler (2010) described a tool called the "Certificate of Confidence" that therapists can use to label, remember, and utilize their unique strengths. This tool invites users to consider the people who first noticed their special strengths and what these were. It encourages users to consider what people appreciate about them now—and to identify others in their networks who also have these characteristics, because spending time with like-minded people helps to nurture important skills and attitudes. A final question asks the therapist to consider the single most important quality or ability to remember when under pressure. Wheeler wrote: "In times at work when you feel like you have lost your footing, it is likely that when you act this particular way, the uniqueness of who you can be has a chance of coming more fully into being" (p. 229).

Another method for using input from others to grow one's proficiency was suggested by Duncan (2010). This tool invites keeping a "treasure chest" of unsolicited cards, notes, and letters from clients. When the therapist reviews and adds to this special collection, it provides an opportunity to reflect about clients who have taught important lessons over the years. The process also creates a continually evolving narrative of one's development as a therapist.

A "RECIPE" FOR FRUSTRATION IN THERAPIST DEVELOPMENT—AND AN ALTERNATIVE

This book has discussed how solutions can be like recipes that contain multiple ingredients. There is, unfortunately, a common "recipe" for training in the solution-focused and strategic therapies that does not contribute to competency at the higher levels. It includes the following "ingredients":

1. Attend a brief training.
2. Learn some techniques and receive some handouts. (Optional: Buy the presenter's book.)
3. Watch the experts (live and/or on video) create amazing miracles and brilliant interventions, seemingly without effort, with difficult clients. (There is no discussion of obstacles that may come up when one tries to "do this at home.")
4. Return to your practice setting. Working in relative isolation, surrounded by colleagues, supervisors, and clinic administrators who use a different model, attempt to duplicate what you just learned. ("Why isn't this working for me like it did for them? It looked so easy. I must not be a very good therapist. This approach isn't as good as I thought it was ...")
5. In the clinical record and case discussions, conceal any attempts to be solution-focused or strategic. (This should be easy to do, since those attempts aren't working very well anyway ...)

The above is intended to be a bit of a caricature. Unfortunately, however, this scenario may occur more frequently than many solution-focused and strategic therapists care to admit. In contrast, in the strategic solution focused spirit of what one does when something is not working well enough, we will consider the following alternate recipe.

In this scenario, one learns solution-focused or strategic therapy together with some colleagues. Training includes anticipation of specific challenges that may emerge in applying the model and some tools for managing them. (An example is, J. Simon's [2010] "When the client doesn't follow the script" exercise, described earlier in this chapter.) Here are some "ingredients" for this recipe:

1. Learn and begin to use solution-focused and strategic tools in a supportive setting, with clinical support from colleagues and supervisors and administrative support for the model from managers.
2. Eagerly elicit feedback from clients (on measures such as Polaris-MH [Polaris Health Directions, 2010]), with "low scores" welcomed as opportunities to discover how and when to do something different.
3. Grow your skills slowly. Incorporate pieces of other methods that are valuable and that work for you and for your clients.

4. Train other therapists and insure that you impart all three of the following: knowledge, procedures, and attitude. Grow your skills together, over time. Welcome trainees who aspire to be clinicians and those who will conduct research on the model.
5. Read about new developments. Attend conferences on solution-focused and strategic practice.
6. Collect data on outcome and therapeutic alliance in solution-focused and strategic therapy. Use that data to fine-tune treatment with practice-based evidence.
7. Write about what you discover and/or conduct research, adding to the evidence base of solution-focused and strategic practice.

The above recipe yields: Clients who discover solutions, therapists who practice at higher levels of competency, and more creative methods in the solution-focused and strategic therapies.

The above scenario might be viewed as the solution-focused or strategic therapist's "miracle" for training and professional growth. It is also one way of describing the conditions that existed both at the Mental Research Institute (MRI) and the Brief Family Therapy Center (BFTC) when the models were developed. In other settings, therapists have created clinics and agencies that use solution-focused and/or strategic methods as the primary approach. Examples include a Northern California Kaiser Permanente clinic that adopted the MRI model (Chubb & Evans, 1987) and a Colorado agency that built a solution-focused practice (Pichot & Dolan, 2003). Many solution-focused and strategic therapists do not have that much support around them, but they can still seek out and create learning communities. After all, solution-focused and strategic therapists know that one does not have to wait for the full, complete miracle to occur in order to notice and amplify pieces of it that are already happening!

At its conclusion, this book—like the strategic solution focused therapist—returns to the basics: doing what works. As discussed throughout, this perspective applies to the client's life, and it works on other levels as well. It is the cornerstone of a flexible strategic solution focused approach, and it is a philosophy shared transparently with clients and trainees alike. Doing what works applies to the therapist's process and ongoing professional development.

In that spirit, the ideas in this chapter invite therapists to grow in multiple ways. Therapists are invited to create new tools for the toolbox. They are invited to notice more ways of listening and leading from behind, with new possibilities for discovering and amplifying client strengths. They are invited to monitor process and outcome, building on what works and modifying what does not. They are invited to actively embrace challenges, to increase flexibility, and to transform impasses into possibilities.

These therapist choices enhance both therapist competence and joy in the work. They support growth in the core *knowledge, skills,* and *attitudes* that characterize solution-focused and strategic practice at the highest levels of competency. They contribute to evidence-based practice, and they make a positive difference for clients, today.

NOTE

1. The Solution-Focused Brief Therapy Organization (http://www.sfbta.org), the MRI (http://www.mri.org), the European Brief Therapy Association (http://www.ebta.nu), and the Brief Strategic and Systemic Therapy Network (http://www.bsst.org) are a few resources for solution-focused and strategic therapists. They offer workshops, books, and some training videos. Some materials from the MRI are available in Spanish.

REFERENCES

Abu Raiya, H., & Pargament, K. (2010). Religiously integrated psychotherapy with Muslim clients: From research to practice. *Professional Psychology: Research and Practice, 41*(2), 181–188.

American Psychiatric Association. (2000). *Diagnostic and statistical manual of mental disorders DSM-IV-TR fourth edition (text revision).* Arlington, VA: American Psychiatric Publishing.

Atherton, J. (2008). *Doceo; competence, proficiency and beyond.* Retrieved from http://www.doceo.co.uk/background/expertise.htm

Avard, P. (2010). Solution-focused brief therapy and watercolors? In T. Nelson (Ed.), *Doing something different: Solution-focused brief therapy practices* (pp. 237–238). New York, NY: Routledge.

Bannick, F. (2007). Solution-focused brief therapy. *Journal of Contemporary Psychotherapy, 37,* 87–94.

Bannink, F. (2010, September). *Bridging solution focus and positive psychology.* Workshop presented at the European Brief Therapy Association Conference, Malmo, Sweden.

Bavelas, J., Gerwing, J., Healing, S., & Tomori, C. (2010, November). *How can I use microanalysis to be a better SF practitioner, trainer, teacher, or supervisor?* Workshop presented at the Solution Focused Brief Therapy Association 2010 Conference, Banff, Alberta, Canada.

Beck, A. (1996). *Beck Depression Inventory II.* San Antonio, TX: The Psychological Corporation.

Berg, I. (Case therapist) (2008). *Irreconcilable differences: A solution-focused approach to marital therapy* [DVD]. Psychotherapy.net.

Berg, I., & de Shazer, S. (1993). Making numbers talk: Language in therapy. In S. Friedman (Ed.), *The new language of change: Constructive collaboration in psychotherapy* (pp. 5–24). New York, NY: Guilford.

Beyebach, M. (2007, September). *Solutions for "stuck cases" in solution-focused therapy.* Workshop presented at the European Brief Therapy Association Conference, Bruges, Belgium.

Bliss, V. (2010). Extreme listening. In T. Nelson (Ed.), *Doing something different: Solution-focused brief therapy practices* (pp. 109–116). New York, NY: Routledge.

Bohart, A., & Talmon, K. (2010). Clients: The neglected common factor in psychotherapy. In B. Duncan, S. Miller, B. Wampold, & M. Hubble (Eds.), *The heart and soul of change: Delivering what works* (2nd ed., pp. 83–112). Washington, DC: American Psychological Association.

Bordin, E. (1979). The generalizability of the psychoanalytic concept of the working alliance. *Psychotherapy, 16,* 252–260.

Boscolo, L., Cecchin, G., Hoffman, L., & Penn, P. (1987). *Milan systemic family therapy: Theoretical and practical aspects.* New York: Harper & Row.

Brehm, J. (1966). *A theory of psychological reactance.* New York, NY: Academic Press.

Cade, B., & O'Hanlon, W. (1993). *A brief guide to brief therapy.* New York, NY: Norton.

Chubb, H., & Evans, E. (1987). *Clinic productivity and accessibility with the Mental Research Institute brief therapy model.* Unpublished manuscript.

Clay, R. (2010). Treating traumatized children. *Monitor on Psychology, 41*(7), 36–39.

Connerly, M., & Pederson, P. (2005). *Leadership in a diverse and multicultural environment: Developing awareness, knowledge, and skills.* Thousand Oaks, CA: Sage.

De Jong, P., & Bavelas, J. (2010, November). *What is different about SFBT?* Plenary session conducted at the Solution Focused Brief Therapy Association 2010 Conference, Banff, Alberta, Canada.

de Shazer, S. (1984). The death of resistance. *Family Process, 23,* 79–93.

de Shazer, S. (1985). *Keys to solution in brief therapy.* New York: Norton.

de Shazer, S. (1988). *Clues: Investigating solutions in brief therapy.* New York, NY: Norton.

de Shazer, S., & Dolan, Y. (with Korman, H., Trepper, T., McCollum, E., & Berg, I.). (2007). *More than miracles: The state of the art of solution-focused brief therapy.* New York, NY: Haworth.

Dobbins, J. (2010, August). Emerging scaffold of evidence-based treatments, diversity, and social responsibility. In N. Kaslow (Chair) *Evidence-based treatments in family psychology: Evaluating the research.* Symposium conducted at the American Psychological Association Conference, San Diego, CA.

Dolan, Y. (1998). *One small step.* Watsonville, CA: Papier-Mache.

Dolan, Y. (2009, November). *Advanced solution-focused listening.* Workshop presented at the Solution Focused Brief Therapy Association Conference, Albany, NY.

Dreyfus, H., & Dreyfus, S. (1986). *Mind over machine.* New York, NY: Free Press.

Duncan, B. (2010). *On becoming a better therapist.* Washington, DC: American Psychological Association.

Duncan, B., Hubble, M., & Miller, S. (1997). *Psychotherapy with "impossible" cases: Efficient treatment of therapy veterans.* New York, NY: Norton.

Duncan, B., Miller, S., Sparks, J., Claud, D., Reynolds, L., Brown, J., & Johnson, L. (2003). The session rating scale: Preliminary properties of a "working" alliance measure. *Journal of Brief Therapy, 3(1),* 3–12.

Ericsson, K. (2000). Expert performance and deliberate practice. An updated excerpt from Ericsson (2000). Retrieved from http://www.psy.fsu.edu/faculty/ericsson/ericsson.exp.perf.html

Fiebelkorn, B., Chesmore, C., Ranney, T., & Vollmer, B. (2010, August). *Collaborative treatment planning: Evaluation of incorporating client preferences.* Poster session presented at the American Psychological Association Convention, San Diego, CA.

Fields, A. (2010). Multicultural research and practice: Theoretical issues and maximizing cultural exchange. *Professional Psychology: Research and Practice, 41*(3), 196–201.

Fisch, R., & Schlanger, K. (1999). *Brief therapy with intimidating cases*. San Francisco, CA: John Wiley & Sons.

Fisch, R., Weakland, J., & Segal, L. (1982). *The tactics of change*. San Francisco, CA: John Wiley & Sons.

Fiske, H. (2008). *Hope in action: Solution-focused conversations about suicide*. New York, NY: Routledge.

Fiske, H. (2009, November). *Hope in action: Solution-focused suicide prevention*. Plenary session conducted at the Solution Focused Brief Therapy Association Conference, Albany, NY.

Freeman, S. (2010). Supervision e-mail from the future. In T. Nelson (Ed.), *Doing something different: Solution-focused brief therapy practices* (pp. 161–166). New York, NY: Routledge.

Funk & Wagnalls. (1966). *Standard college dictionary*. New York: Funk & Wagnalls.

Gassman, D., & Grawe, K. (2006). General change mechanisms: The relation between problem activation and resource activation in successful and unsuccessful therapeutic interactions. *Clinical Psychology and Psychotherapy, 13*, 1–11.

George, E., Iveson, C., Ratner, H., & Shennan, G. (2009). *BRIEFER: A Solution-focused practice manual*. London, England: BRIEF.

Gorden, B. (2010a). The artful diagnostician. In T. Nelson (Ed.), *Doing something different: Solution-focused brief therapy Practices* (pp. 167–170). New York, NY: Routledge.

Gorden, B. (2010b). The worst things you could ever hear in a therapy hour. In T. Nelson (Ed.), *Doing something different: Solution-focused brief therapy practices* (pp. 193–196). New York, NY: Routledge.

Haley, J. (1973). *Uncommon therapy*. New York, NY: Ballantine Books.

Hayes, H. (1991). The "Zen" lady: An interview with Insoo Kim Berg. *Australian and New Zealand Journal of Family Therapy, 12*, 155–158.

Kaslow, N. (2004). Competencies in professional psychology. *American Psychologist, 59*, 774–781.

Kiesler, D. (2001). Therapist countertransference: In search of common themes and empirical referents. *Journal of Clinical Psychology, 57*(8), 1053–1063.

Kleckner, T., Frank, L., Bland, C., & Amendt, J. (1992). The myth of the unfeeling strategic therapist. *Journal of Marital and Family Therapy, 18*, 41–51.

Kluckhohn, C. (1951). The study of culture. In D. Lerner & H. Laswell (Eds.), *The policy sciences* (pp. 86–101). Stanford, CA: Stanford University Press.

Knapp, S., & VandeCreek, L. (2006). *Practical ethics for psychologists: A positive approach*. Washington, DC: American Psychological Association.

Korman, H. (2010). Psychiatry should be a parenthesis in people's lives. In T. Nelson (Ed.), *Doing something different: Solution-focused brief therapy practices* (pp. 209–212). New York, NY: Routledge.

Krishnamurthy, R., VandeCreek, L., Kaslow, N., Tazeau, Y., Miville, M., Kerns, R., Stegman, R., Suzuki, L., & Benton, S. (2004). Achieving competency in psychological assessment: Directions for education and training. *Journal of Clinical Psychology, 60*(7), 725–739.

177

Lambert, M. (1992). Psychotherapy outcome research: Implications for integrative and eclectic therapists. In J. Norcross & M. Goldfried, (Eds.), *Handbook of psychotherapy integration* (pp. 94–129). New York, NY: Basic Books.

Linehan, M. (1993). *Cognitive behavioral treatment of borderline personality disorders.* New York, NY: Guilford.

Linehan, M., Goodstein J., Nielsen S., & Chiles, J. (1983). Reasons for staying alive when you are thinking of killing yourself: The Reasons for Living Inventory. *Journal of Consulting and Clinical Psychology, 51,* 276–286.

Lipchik, E. (1994). The rush to be brief. *Family Therapy Networker, 18*(2), 35–39.

Lipchik, E. (2002). *Beyond technique in solution-focused therapy: Working with emotions and the therapeutic relationship.* New York, NY: Guilford.

Lopez, S. (2009, January). *Shifting cultural lenses in clinical practice.* Workshop presented at Kaiser Permanente Education Meeting, San Diego.

Macdonald, A. (2010, September). *An overview of outcome studies in solution-focused therapy.* Panel discussion presentation at the European Brief Therapy Association Conference, Malmo, Sweden.

Marlatt, G., & Gordon, J. (1985). *Relapse prevention: Maintenance and strategies in the treatment of addictive behaviors.* New York, NY: Guilford.

McKergow, M. (2010, September). *SF coaching for leaders.* Plenary session conducted at the European Brief Therapy Association Conference, Malmo, Sweden.

Metcalf, L. (2001). Solution focused therapy. In R. Corsini (Ed.), *Handbook of innovative therapy* (2nd ed., pp. 647–659). New York, NY: John Wiley & Sons.

Miller, S. (Case therapist) (1999). *Brief therapy inside out: Client directed interaction: Adjusting the therapy not the person* [VHS]. Phoenix, AZ: Zeig, Tucker, & Co.

Miller, S. (2008, December). *Supershrinks: Learning from the most effective practitioners.* Workshop presented at the Milton Erickson Conference, San Diego, CA.

Miller, S., Duncan, B., Brown, J., Sparks, J., & Claud, D. (2003). The outcome rating scale: A preliminary study of the reliability, validity, and feasibility of a brief visual analog measure. *Journal of Brief Therapy, 2(2),* 91–100.

Miller, S., Norcross, J., Polster, E., & Prochaska, J. (2008, December). *Setting goals in brief therapy.* Panel discussion presented at the Milton Erickson Conference, San Diego, CA.

MRI.org. (2010). *Mental Research Institute: Brief therapy.* Retrieved from http://www.mri.org/brief_therapy.html

Nardone, G. & Portelli, C. (2005). *Knowing through changing: The evolution of brief strategic therapy.* Norwalk, CT: Crown House Publishing.

Nardone, G., & Watzlawick, P. (1993). *The art of change: Strategic therapy and hypnotherapy without trance.* San Francisco, CA: John Wiley & Sons.

Norcross, J. (2005, April). *Tailoring the therapeutic relationship to the individual patient: Evidence-based practices.* Workshop presented at Kaiser Permanente Education Meeting, San Diego.

Nylund, D., & Corsiglia, V. (1994). Becoming solution (focused) forced in brief therapy: Remembering something important we already knew. *Journal of Systemic Therapies, 13,* 5–11.

O'Hanlon, W., & Weiner-Davis, M. (1989). *In search of solutions.* New York, NY: Norton.

Olsson, P., & Wennerholm, M. (2010, September). *Is the miracle scale a key to understand dropouts?* Paper presented at the European Brief Therapy Association Conference, Malmo, Sweden.

Orlinsky, D., & Rønnestad, M. (2005). *How psychotherapists develop: A study of therapeutic work and professional growth.* Washington, DC: American Psychological Association.

Orlinsky, D., Rønnestad, M., & Willutzki, U. (2003). Fifty years of process-outcome research: Continuity and change. In M. J. Lambert (Ed.), *Bergin and Garfield's handbook of psychotherapy and behavior change* (5th ed., pp. 307–390). New York, NY: John Wiley & Sons.

Panayotov, P. (2010, September). *Simple therapy: A step beyond.* Workshop presented at the European Brief Therapy Association Conference, Malmo, Sweden.

Peterson, C., & Seligman, M. (2004). *Character strengths and virtues.* Washington, DC: American Psychological Association Press & Oxford University Press.

Pichot, T., & Dolan, Y. (2003). *Solution-focused brief therapy: Its effective use in agency settings.* New York, NY: Routledge.

Plante, T. (2010). *Contemporary clinical psychology.* Hoboken, NJ: John Wiley & Sons.

Polaris Health Directions. (2010, September 13). Polaris–MH. Retrieved from http://www.polarishealth.com/solutions/MH/mental_health.html

Prochaska, J., & DiClemente, C. (1992). *The transtheoretical approach.* New York, NY: Basic Books.

Quick, E. (2007). *A qualitative analysis of pilot IITP follow-up questionnaire response data.* Unpublished manuscript, Department of Psychiatry and Addiction Medicine, Kaiser Permanente, San Diego.

Quick, E. (2008). *Doing what works in brief therapy: A strategic solution focused approach* (2nd ed.). San Diego, CA: Elsevier.

Quick, E. (2010a, September). *The classics and the hybrids in the solution-focused community.* Workshop presented at the European Brief Therapy Association, Malmo, Sweden.

Quick, E. (2010b, February). *The doing what works approach to solution focused therapy.* Solution Focused Mastercourse, Amsterdam, The Netherlands.

Quick, E., & Gizzo, D. (2007). The doing what works group: A quantitative and qualitative analysis of solution focused group therapy. *Journal of Family Psychotherapy, 18*(3), 65–85.

Rønnestad, M., & Skovholt, T. (2003). The journey of the counselor and therapist: Research findings and perspectives on professional development. *Journal of Career Development, 30*(1), 5–44.

Ruesh, R., & Bateson, G. (1951). *Communication: The social matrix of psychiatry.* New York, NY: Norton.

Schön, D. (1983). *The reflective practitioner.* New York: Basic Books.

Segal, L. (2001). Brief therapy. In R. Corsini (Ed.), *Handbook of innovative therapy* (2nd ed., pp. 86–94). New York, NY: John Wiley & Sons.

179

Short, D. (1997). Interview, Steve de Shazer and Insoo Kim Berg. *Milton Erickson Foundation Newsletter, 17*(2), 1, 18–20.

Simon, D. (1993). Random notes/First word. *News of the Difference, 2*(3), 1.

Simon, J. (2010). When the client doesn't follow the script. In T. Nelson (Ed.), *Doing something different: Solution-focused brief therapy practices* (pp. 213–216). New York, NY: Routledge.

Simon, J. & Nelson, T., Eds. (2007). *Solution-focused brief practice with long term clients in mental health services: I am more than my label.* New York: Haworth.

Smock, S. (2010). Evidence-based supervision: Identifying successful moments of Solution-focused brief therapy. In T. Nelson (Ed.), *Doing something different: Solution-focused brief therapy practices* (pp. 97–200). New York, NY: Routledge.

Smock, S. (2011). A review of solution focused, standardized outcome measures and other strengths oriented outcome measures. In C. Franklin, T. Trepper, W. Gingerich, & E. McCollum (Eds.), *Solution-focused brief therapy.* New York, NY: Oxford University Press.

Sperry, L. (2010a). *Core competencies in counseling and psychotherapy: Becoming a highly competent and effective therapist.* New York, NY: Routledge.

Sperry L. (2010b). *Highly effective therapy: Developing essential clinical competencies in counseling and psychotherapy.* New York, NY: Routledge.

Storm, C. (1991). The remaining thread: Matching change and stability signals. *Journal of Strategic and Systemic Therapies, 10,* 114–117.

Stricker, G., & Trierweiler, S. (1995). The local clinical scientist: A bridge between science and practice. *American Psychologist, 50,* 995–1002.

Trepper, T., McCollum, E., De Jong, P., Korman, H., Gingerich, W., & Franklin, C. (2010, April 10). *Solution focused therapy treatment manual for working with individuals.* Retrieved from http://www.sfbta.org/research.pdf

Trepper, T., Treyger, S., & Yalowitzh, J. (2007, November). *Solution focused sex therapy.* Workshop presented at the Solution Focused Brief Therapy Association Conference, Toronto, Canada.

Wampold, B. (2007). Psychotherapy: The humanistic (and effective) treatment. *American Psychologist, 62*(8), 857–887.

Watzlawick, P. (1992, December). *The creation of "reality" through language.* Workshop presented at the Milton Erickson Conference, Phoenix, AZ.

Watzlawick, P., Weakland, J., & Fisch, R. (1974). *Change: Principles of problem formation and problem resolution.* New York, NY: Norton.

Weakland, J. (1978). OK—You've been a bad mother. In P. Papp (Ed.), *Family therapy full length case studies* (pp. 23–33). New York, NY: Garden Press.

Weakland, J., Fisch, R., Watzlawick, P., & Bodin, A. (1974). Brief therapy: Focused problem resolution. *Family Process, 13,* 141–167.

Wheeler, J. (2010). Certificate of competence. In T. Nelson (Ed.), *Doing something different: Solution-focused brief therapy practices* (pp. 225–232). New York, NY: Routledge.

Yalom, V., & Rubin, B. (2010, October 31). *An interview with Insoo Kim Berg, LCSW.* Retrieved from http://www.psychotherapy.net/interview/insoo-kim-berg

INDEX